QING IMPERIAL COSTUME DESIGN:

YIN-YANG PHILOSOPHICAL INFLUENCES

清宮珍藏龍袍

羅錦堂

夏威夷大學
中國文化收藏品

QING IMPERIAL COSTUME DESIGN:
YIN-YANG PHILOSOPHICAL INFLUENCES

Shu-Hwa Lin, Ph.D.

**Artifacts from the Asian Costume Collection
at the University of Hawaiʻi at Mānoa and the Honolulu Museum of Art**

The University of Hawai'i at Mānoa Costume Collection consists of approximately 20,000 garments, textiles and artifacts from various regions of the world. All items in the collection have been specially donated to the Apparel Design and Merchandising Program, University of Hawai'i at Mānoa (UHM).

This text features six Qing imperial costumes from the University of Hawai'i Asian Costume Collection and four Qing imperial costumes from the Honolulu Museum of Art.

Special thanks to our project participants:
Dr. Wei Ye, Sara Oka, Chelsea Duarte, Kelly Mammel, Shing Yan Lo,
Becky Tong, Mandy Ho, Constantinos Vrakas, Pete Hsu, Sun Xing,
Ryan Cho, Tee Pham, Christen Ige, Anthony Diep.
Book design and typographic composition by Daniel Tschudi.

Calligraphy on frontispiece and pages 20, 30, 32, 49, and 68 by University of Hawai'i at Mānoa emeritus professor Chin-tang Lo. Title page calligraphy of the Chinese character *long* ('dragon'), collection of Chin-tang Lo. Attributed to the Qing Xuantong Emperor.
Front cover: Dragon medallion with sun bird symbol from *gunfu* robe.
Back cover: Dragon medallion with moon symbol from *gunfu* robe.

First Published in 2013
by Department of Family and Consumer Sciences
2515 Campus Rd., Miller Hall 110, University of Hawai'i at Mānoa
Honolulu, HI 96822 USA

© 2013 Shu-Hwa Lin
ISBN: 978-0-9886470-0-8

CONTENTS

Funding to support this project was provided by the Hawai'i Council for the Humanities and the Department of Family and Consumer Sciences, College of Tropical Agriculture and Human Resources, University of Hawai'i at Mānoa.

PREFACE 序

Due to successive waves of immigration from mainland China over the past two centuries, a good number of Chinese court costumes have been collected by major museums and universities around the world, including the Auckland War Memorial Museum and the University of Hawai'i at Mānoa (UHM). I was recently honored to be invited to visit the Asia collection workrooms at the Auckland War Memorial Museum. Secretary Tracey Wedge and museum curator Rose Young arranged my tour through the New Zealand Costume & Textile Section at the Auckland Museum Institute. It was truly a joy to examine one of the newest additions to the collection, a four-clawed python robe, as the new dragon robe and I arrived at the War Memorial Museum on the same day.

Many studies of Chinese court costume have revealed that complex social arrangements, such as imperial kinship and civil or military official codes, were indicated by court dress. Fernald (1946), for example, indicated which specific characters were used as ornamental designs in Chinese court costumes. Cammann (1952) provided details of complex dragon robes and Scott (1958) dealt with Chinese theatrical costumes. Capon (1970) illustrated Chinese court robes in several collections of articles and paintings for exhibition. Vollmer (1977a, 1977b) explained court robe construction and symbols and also depicted (1983) the status of dragon robes as garments and symbols of patterns. Court dragon robes have been very important and valuable collections for researchers to explore how the ancient Chinese used textiles to demonstrate political power and social rank, and to reconstruct historical Chinese textile technology.

Patterns are woven into silk damasks, brocades, velvets, and tapestries, plus embroidered or appliquéd onto the fabric surface. Weavers produced slit tapestries, or *kesi* (緙絲), to create complex patterns and pictorial scenes in the Qing Dynasty (Shih, 1977; Vollmer, 1977a). Slit tapestry is defined as "formed by the filling yarns, which are interlaced back and forth through warp yarns only where needed instead of completed across the fabric" (Tortora & Merkel, 1996, p. 563). Satin and leno were also commonly used methods in Chinese silk fabrics (Harris, 2004; Rebound, 1977). Embroidery stitches were one of the methods to be adapted to create complex motifs in the Qing Dynasty, such as French knots. Some patterns have assigned meaning to indicate the wearer's social status.

The purpose of this project was to analyze how Qing dragon robe artifacts demonstrate political power and social rank, and to examine ten examples of dragon robes and other Chinese garments dating from the late 19th century to the early 20th century. The primary analysis was the use of color, material, pattern, and garment type to indicate rank and social status. The weave structures of major fabrics (satin, slit tapestry, and leno weave) were also selected for analysis. The

textiles were analyzed using linen testers, visual examination, and artifact documents. Also, yarn structures (i.e., single, ply), fabric structures (i.e., satin, tapestry, leno weaves), and embroidery stitches were examined. The results of this research can be used to develop research strategies for Chinese cultural artifacts of both the past and present.

Much has been written on Qing designation theory. The expression of rank in design has received little attention, although its rich diversity in color, form, and material offers treasures and intrigue for costume research. This report includes the design rules for official costumes used by the Qing Dynasty to designate rank. This volume examines and analyzes nine dragon robes and one Daoist priest's robe from University of Hawaiʻi at Mānoa Asian Costume Collection and the Honolulu Museum of Art. The analysis was assisted by examining Qing law books such as the *Da Qing Hui Dian Shi Li* 大清會典事例 at the National Central Library of Taipei and *Si Ku Quan Shu* 四庫全書 at University of Hawaiʻi at Mānoa Library.

The use of motifs and the total number of dragons and their claws in the robes were used to identify the rank of the wearer. The application of yarn, fabric, and colors formed the design motifs. For example, the front-facing (seated) dragon is defined as the appearance of a dragon face completely surrounded by a dragon body. A seated dragon is placed at the center of the front and back panels of the robe. The walking dragon design shows a profile of a dragon's face with its body and limbs positioned in a walking posture. A pair of walking dragons is positioned at the shoulders and two sides of the bottom. The detail of the claws could suggest the rank of the wearer. The simplified or less detailed of the dragons could be called pythons, either three-clawed or four-clawed. According to the *Da Qing Hui Dian*, nine four-clawed pythons on blue robes designate third- and fourth-degree princes, imperial dukes, and other nobles. Six of the nine robes were determined to be nine five-clawed dragons on robes, and designate first- and second-degree princes. The use of the dragon was restricted in the Qing Dynasty.

Satin, slit tapestry, rib and leno weaves were found in these dragon robes. Slit tapestry presents complex motifs woven in these fabrics. Sometimes, satin and leno weaves added two or more solid colors in the construction of a dragon robe by using colored threads to create the dragons, eight Buddhist treasures, and twelve sovereignty symbols motifs. A total of nine embroidery stitches were found in these dragon robes, including foundation stitches, holding stitches, thin line stitches, superimposed linear effects, superimposed stitching, couching, and padded embroidery. Both single and ply yarns were found in the fabric of the panels and embroidery threads. For each robe, from four to fourteen colored embroidery threads were used to create rich symbols and motifs.

緣 It has been my great honor to have the opportunity to work on Chinese imperial costumes. As a woman and due to social hierarchies at the time, it would not have been possible for me to work on this project one hundred years ago during the Qing Dynasty reign. My mother's grand-father obtained a *xiucai* 秀才 degree, having passed a local civil service entrance examination and subsequent imperial examinations to obtain higher social standing in the late Qing Dynasty. Yet, even having a relative with such an illustrious pedigree, if it had not been for all the changes within the past century to the modern day, I would not have been allowed to study imperial costumes for this project.

With much encouragement and the support of Dr. Rosita P. Chang, Director, Center for Chinese Studies (CCS); Diane Perushek, Associate Director, CCS; and Daniel Tschudi, Coordinator, CCS, I was able to take my first steps into the manifestation of this project. As a special favor, University of Hawai'i at Mānoa (UHM) Professor Emeritus Dr. Chin-Tang Lo provided his expert penmanship to write the Chinese calligraphy in

dedication to this project. I also thank Professor A. C. Yao, who contributed a special section describing design elements on the Honolulu Museum of Art Daoist priest robe. As part of their research collaboration on this project, UHM Apparel Design and Mechandising Program (APDM) students participated in a field study in China, during which time they attended seminars given by Peking University History Department faculty member Dr. Wei Ye, to whom I also extend my heartfelt thanks.

易 In the early 1970s I took a Chinese philosophy course on the *Yijing* (易經) as an elective, long before I studied Chinese costume history during my undergraduate years.

The *Yijing*, also known as '*I-Ching*,' '*Classic of Changes*' or '*Book of Changes*,' comprises a divination system to explain the operations of the universe. After years of research, I fell in love with the *yin-yang* concept in Chinese costume design theory. As a Chinese textile scientist and functional apparel designer, I have explored the concept of Chinese design theory to realize how important the concept of balance and harmony as realized in the *yin-yang* philosophy is and how it has such a great effect on all aspects of Chinese culture, including food, medicine, and clothing design.

As a young child experiencing the world, the ideas of *yin-yang* were constant influences in my environment. Cultural festivals, at which *yin-yang* faces (a face that is half white and half black) and eyes were prevalent, provided my first encounter with the *yin-yang* concept. In Taiwan, Daoist temples often held large festivals for which people dressed in elaborate costumes and masks to assume different personas to teach lessons to the community. Some masks represented power and guardianship or estimable professions (e.g., scribe). The *yin-yang* mask, with contrasting colors characteristics, embodied justice. *Yin-yang* faces often warned children and lay people to be good and law-abiding. *Yin-yang* eyes (where one eye is different from the other) exaggerated the watchful gaze. These concepts are prevalent in the facial and bodily designs of the UHM and Hawaii Museum of Art (HMA) costumes.

I have found that *yin-yang* philosophy was influential in the design of Chinese court apparel, as is apparent in most of the Qing Dynasty costumes housed in the Asian Costume Collection at UHM. Over the past year, I have been invited to review the Chinese imperial costume collections at several universities

(i.e., Florida State University, University of Rhode Island, and Tainan National University of the Arts, in Taiwan), museums (i.e., the Honolulu Museum of Art, Auckland War Memorial Museum), and have been a guest speaker on the topic at private and public events.

When I was attending Auburn University during the period 1989–1994, I was shown many valuable Chinese costumes and interior household and decorative items, and had further opportunity to exercise the study of Chinese design theory. I was fortunate to be able to peruse the vast collection of Chinese costume literature in the private library of Drs. Pamela Ulrich and France Duffield, at Auburn University. They were very kind to loan me several of these priceless records so that I could continue my avid study of Chinese costume.

I have been invited to critique Chinese dragon robes on many occasions by Dorothy Wells (Florida State University Costume Curator; 1995), Jan Loverin (Marjorie Russell Clothing & Textile Research Center, NV; 2007), and Auckland Museum (Auckland, New Zealand; 2007).

As a Chinese textile scholar and native Chinese speaker, I was requested by Bishop Museum in Honolulu to prepare and translate several Chinese papers into English. This service was for Bishop Museum's exhibition "Celebrating Chinese Women: Qing Dynasty to Modern Hawaii" (2006). This unique exhibition caught the attention of both scholars and the general public because this was the first time such costumes had been released from Beijing's Palace Museum and put on display for public viewing. Textiles were also brought in from the Chinese Costume Museum of Donghua University in Shanghai for this exhibit.

I was invited to view additional important textiles while touring Nevada State Museum. I met Curator Jan Loverin at a meeting of the Costume Society of America in San Diego in 2007, where she invited me to join her at the Marjorie Russell Clothing & Textile Research Center for a special after-hours viewing of important textiles held at the museum. During the visit, I was able to share conservation tips and new field developments with her.

學 In 2006, a group of students from National Pingtung University of Science and Technology, Taiwan, requested to view the UHM Chinese dragon robes during my lecture on Hawaiian tapa after learning that the UHM costume collection owned several prominent artifacts. Therefore, at the suggestion of UHM College of Tropical Agriculture and Human Resources (CTAHR) Associate Dean Dr. C. Y. Hu, I arranged a showing of the Chinese imperial costumes to the Chinese visiting students. His idea was that the experience would demonstrate to these Chinese students the value of their heritage and the importance and wide-spread appeal of Chinese cultural artifacts throughout the world.

練 In the summer 2009, I attended a University of Rhode Island (URI) textile conservation class offered through the Textile Fashion Merchandising and Design Department. The instructor, Dr. Margaret T. Ordoñez, is an expert on foundational and advanced knowledge concerning textile conservation practices and textile chemistry. Dr. Ordonez has taught me many advanced skills and has provided useful advice on multiple occasions. The Costume Collection at URI contains many valuable Chinese costumes and artifacts. This special training reinforced my knowledge about the conservation of historic and ethnographic textiles and clothing.

I have explored Chinese official costume very intensively since 2004. During the past seven years, I have visited Taiwan and China more than eight times. During the research trips, I visited museums to view Chinese imperial costumes and exchanged knowledge with experts in addition to studying eight times at the Palace Museum and National History Museum in Taiwan. I also visited major Qing Dynasty imperial costume collections in China, including the silk museums in Hangzhou, Suzhou, and Nanjing.

Due to the priceless value of Chinese imperial artifacts, I had at least ten officials accompany me while I viewed the Chinese imperial costumes when I was studying at the Palace Museum in Taipei, in 2011. While I was in Taipei, I made great connections while visiting the artifacts at the National History Museum, which houses a large quantity of Chinese imperial costumes. This research was sponsored by the Taipei Economic and Cultural Office in Honolulu.

In the summer of 2010, I was honored to be selected as a UHM–Peking University (PKU) exchange scholar. Peking University has a proud history of traditional liberal arts academics. While I was at PKU, I conducted research with History Department faculty member Dr. Ye Wei. Dr. Ye has greatly contributed to this project on Qing Dynasty Imperial Costumes.

While I was on the exchange program, many educators at PKU found my teaching methods to be beneficial and important to the study of Chinese textiles. I also visited *kesi* 緙絲 (Chinese slit-tapestry) experts. Professor Shao Xiaocheng 邵晓琤 showed me her *kesi* techniques, new replicas, and her antique collections. During that same stay, I also visited two Chinese minority costume museums, Beijing Institute of Fashion Technology and Minzu University of China. I was also able to visit the cities where imperial official robes were made during the Ming and Qing dynas-

ties, including the production sites that are now the Hangzhou Silk Museum, Suzhou Silk Museum, and Nanjing Silk Museum.

This project started from studying and building Chinese textile structure in replica of artifacts from UHM's Asian Costume Collection. A CTAHR startup fund provided me with the ability to hire student employees to create graphic images and video and textile structures in study of the collection's artifacts.

With the help of my student employees' tireless workmanship, this project has been transformed from an abstract contract to a visual and physical reality. I express my greatest appreciation to everyone who participated in this project and especially to the members of my student help group, who worked diligently and contributed their highest efforts. I was very lucky to have so many wonderful student assistants. A very special thanks goes to Chelsea Duarte, Kelly Mammel, and Anthony Diep. Kelly Mammel has worked for me since she was an undergraduate student and continues to contribute her dedicated work during her studies for a postgraduate degree. Chelsea Duarte has been a special person in this project who participated pre- and post-graduation. She participated by editing all graphics and text, and even lent her voice to narrate on the related video project, *Threads of Majesty* (2009). She has been a significant contributor in this project. Without all of the students' efforts, this project would not have been possible.

I must also thank Sara Oka, Curator of Textiles of the Honolulu Museum of Art, for her support, help, and friendship. Ever since we met, we have freely shared our knowledge of costume and design theory. Her support has been indispensible for the success of this project.

Also my heartfelt thanks to Dr. Margaret T. Ordoñez, Dr. Rayneld M. Johnson and Dr. Theresa Sull for their suggestions and comments.

This project would not have been possible without the generous financial support of the Hawai'i Council for Humanities; the Department of Family & Consumer Sciences, the Women's Campus Club, and the Center for Chinese Studies, University of Hawai'i at Mānoa.

With my ongoing collaborative research projects and planned publications, I anticipate that Chinese textile research will continue to grow. Collaborative research involving Chinese textile design and development with Peking University and Minzu University in China, and Chinese Culture University and National Tainan University in Taiwan, will help the CTAHR Asian Costume Collection develop a global Chinese textile research focus. I will also continue to explore themes and subjects related to Chinese textiles with the Honolulu Museum of Art. Results from this research will be incorporated into my textile classes and will help my students to understand culture awareness in Hawaii's local Chinese community and other areas in the Pacific. My scholarly activities in conferences and publications have and will continue to help give the University, the Department of Family & Consumer Sciences, the Asian Costume Collection, and the APDM Program increased visibility.

Shu Hwa Lin, Ph.D.
Associate Professor and
UHM Asian Costume Collection Curator
Apparel Design and Merchandising Program
University of Hawai'i at Mānoa
2004–present

The first time I saw the dragon robe collection, in 2007, I was moved by the beauty of these ancient garments and thought to myself, "These are truly treasures!" At the time, I was the director of the Center for Chinese Studies at the University of Hawai'i at Mānoa. Dr. Shu-Hwa Lin, who is well known for her expertise in textiles, had invited me to view these rare costumes. They ranged from gorgeous and intricately designed imperial robes (*gunfu*) to court gowns (*jifu* or dragon robes) and ladies costumes. Over the years, members of Hawaii's Chinese and non-Chinese community had donated them to the Department of Family and Consumer Sciences at UH Mānoa, where Lin is now an associate professor.

However, due to years of neglect, some of the pieces were in various stages of degradation and needed extensive restoration work. Since Professor Lin joined UHM in 2004, she has taken on a one-woman crusade to restore the dragon robe collection, which includes more than ten items.

Over the last few years, the Center for Chinese Studies has supported the mission to restore the robes and created ways to showcase them. In our first project, we printed a packet of note cards, featuring twelve costumes from the collection.

This book, *Yin-Yang Philosophical Influences on Chinese Imperial Costume Design,* and its companion DVD, represents Professor Lin and her students' latest efforts to preserve these costumes and help educate people about the Qing Dynasty (1644–1911), China's last imperial dynasty, founded by the Manchu people.

I would like to thank Professor Lin for her dedication and passion in preserving the dragon robe collection and communicating its unique value and importance to the rest of the world. She has been a leader in a group of researchers, artists, and scholars who are conducting research projects on Chinese imperial costumes with her new approach of creating various media publications (CD and booklet) suitable for both the public and academic community.

I sincerely hope that one day we can all look forward to seeing these magnificent garments restored once again to their original splendor and on display at the Mānoa campus for everyone to enjoy.

Rosita P. Chang, Ph.D.
Chair and Professor of Finance
Director, Center for Chinese Studies, 2006–'09
University of Hawai'i at Mānoa

It is my pleasure to provide this introduction for an important book that documents the "*Yin-Yang* Philosophical Influences on Chinese Imperial Costume Design." The University of Hawai'i at Mānoa, Department of Family and Consumer Sciences, Historic Costume Collection has been described as a hidden treasure and is preserved for costume and cultural historians (2009 Hawai'i State Legislative Session resolutions to support the UHM Costume Collection-SR57, SCR92, HR101, HCR122). The Costume Collection contains approximately 15,000 ethnographic costume artifacts, and the sub-Asian collection contains between 4,000 to 8,000 Asian textile and costume artifacts. The present book documents how *yin-yang* philosophy influenced Chinese imperial costume and dragon robe design in the Qing Dynasty.

This research project was funded by the Hawai'i Council for the Humanities; College of Tropical Agriculture and Human Resources and Department of Family and Consumer Sciences, the Center for Chinese Studies, and the Women's Campus Club at the University of Hawai'i at Mānoa; Honolulu Museum of Art (formerly Honolulu Academy of Arts); and Taipei Economic and Cultural Office in Honolulu, 2011. This book documents Dr. Lin's research to investigate the *yin-yang* influences on Qing Dynasty Chinese imperial costumes and antique Chinese textiles. Dr. Lin's interest in Chinese philosophy began with an elective *I-Ching* course as an undergraduate. This interest in Chinese philosophy has evolved into an examination of how *yin-yang* philosophical concepts were woven into and illustrated in Chinese imperial costume design. During the course of conducting research for this book, Dr. Lin examined imperial costumes from the Costume Collection at the University of Hawai'i at Mānoa, Honolulu Museum of Art, and across the globe.

Since 2004, Dr. Lin has taken every opportunity to research and examine Chinese textiles and imperial costumes. She started with a close examination of the Chinese official costumes in the Chinese collection at the University of Hawai'i at Mānoa. She was the Chinese textiles consultant and translator for the Bishop Museum in April 2006 for their "Celebrating Chinese Women: Qing Dynasty to Modern Hawaii" exhibit. Dr. Lin was able to examine Chinese costumes from the Imperial Palace Museum in Beijing and Donghua University in Shanghai. In June 2007, Dr. Lin analyzed Chinese textiles and Dragon Robe conservation tips, and shared her knowledge with the curators of Nevada State Museum's Marjorie Russell Clothing and Textile Research Center. In 2005 and again in 2010, she conducted research on their Chinese textiles with a digital microscope and documented detailed fiber and weave structures. She shared these findings with staff from the Honolulu Musem of Art (HMA), which has led to several collaborative efforts with Sara Oka, HMA Curator of Textiles.

Dr. Lin has traveled to Taiwan and the People's Republic of China more than eight times to visit the Imperial Palace Museum in Bejing and National History Museum in Taiwan. She also visited and conducted research in Chinese cities (silk cities) that produced the imperial robes during the Ming and Qing dynasties. The Hangzhou Silk, Suzhou Silk, and Nanjing Silk museums contained numerous examples of textiles and costumes from this time period. Research trips to other museums that were once production sites for the fabrication of Chinese dragon robes included two Chinese minority costume museums, Beijing Institute of Fashion Technology, and Central Nationality University (now Minzu University), in Beijing, China (2010, 2011, 2012). Dr. Lin has been invited as a consultant on Chinese textiles for the Auckland War Memorial Museum and was invited to speak on Chinese imperial costume design at University of Rhode Island and in Tainan Arts University's Fiber Arts Graduate Program, in Tainan, Taiwan. She has also served as a juror of the Mandarin garment contest since 2009 for the Hawai'i Chinese Civic Association, Honolulu.

Several Chinese imperial costume and dragon robe research collaborations have been established. For example, Dr. Lin was selected as a UHM-Peking University (PKU) exchange scholar in the summer of 2010, and conducted research with Dr. Ye Wei, a professor in the History Department, PKU. Professor Ye has been one of the contributors to this project on Qing Dynasty imperial costumes. Future collaborations were sparked while Dr. Lin visited other universities and textile and apparel manufacturers/companies in China. She learned innovative ways to perform research and conduct courses from her colleagues at the universities in China. She brought back these teaching and research methods to UHM as well as reciprocating by sharing her teaching methods and research interests with multiple professors in China. Professor Ma from Minzu University has requested a future opportunity to work with Dr. Lin as a visiting scholar in the future.

Analysis of the *yin-yang* concept from Qing Dynasty imperial costumes design theory together with detailed description of the artifacts reveal exquisite textile technologies and complex design motifs that symbolize political power and social ranking. As a result of the extensive research for this project, the book scientifically examines textile characteristics and Qing Dynasty culture as reflected in dress and apparel. This book will be a an important vehicle to document and share some of the research findings on our unique Qing Dynasty costumes housed at the University of Hawai'i at Mānoa and in the Honolulu Art Museum Costume Collection.

Examples of Dr. Lin's refereed publications, presentations, and multimedia products such as CDs from this research project are noted below.

We look forward to future Chinese costume research publications, presentations, and collaborations from researchers around the world exploring the "*Yin-Yang* Philosophical Influences on Chinese Imperial Costume Design" and other fascinating research on the treasures in the University of Hawai'i at Mānoa Costume Collection.

Barbara W. K. Yee, Ph.D.
Professor and Chair
Department of Family and Consumer Sciences
College of Tropical Agriculture and Human Resources
University of Hawai'i at Mānoa

Lin, S. (July-October, 2007). "Expressions of political rank by textiles: Historic Chinese dragon robes." *Context,* 13, 23–27.

Lin, S. (March-June 2008). "Chinese court dress design principles." *Context,* 15, 12–15.

Lin, S. (2009). Digitization video of Chinese last empire dress code. In J. Thompson, A. Holden, G. Petersen, & S. Stevens (eds.), *Textile Conservation Special Group Special Edition,* Postprint, American Institution for Conservation, 19, 180–183.

Lin, S., (2009). *Threads of majesty: Qing imperial costume collection.* Center of Chinese Studies & Department of Family & Consumer Sciences, University of Hawai'i at Mānoa. (Running time: 27:02 minutes).

Lin, S., (2009). *Weaving political power: UH Qing imperial costume collection.* Center of Chinese Studies & Department of Family & Consumer Sciences, University of Hawai'i at Mānoa.

Lin, S. (2010). "Yin & Yang: Uncovering the messages behind three imperial dragon robes." Oral presentation, Second International Congress on Chinese Studies Urban Society; Spain.

It was a great honor and privilege to work with Dr. Lin on *Chasing The Flaming Pearl,* a recent exhibition of Chinese textiles from the collection here at the Honolulu Museum of Art. Dr. Lin was instrumental in providing a discriminating analysis of the *yin-yang* influences found on the imperial robes. Together, we made revealing discoveries that had previously gone unnoticed. A closer look at color changes, motif alterations, composition, and placement as well as the combinations of elements, revealed how all played a critical role in how these influences were interpreted. We spent endless hours counting dragons, dragon toes, dragon legs, pearls, flames, bats, swastikas and other symbols, all the while looking for patterns, commonalities, differences and distinctions. Along the way we each gained an even greater appreciation and profound admiration for the makers of these exquisite textiles. The superb photography by our HMA staff photographer, Shuzo Uemoto, also enriched the discoveries we made by highlighting some of the intricate details that were otherwise barely discernable by eye. These garments stand as testament to the complexity of power and prestige bestowed upon the wearers of these majestic costumes.

Sara Oka
Curator of Textiles
Honolulu Museum of Art

INTRODUCTION 龍

The Qing Dynasty (1644–1911) was the last ruling dynasty of China. Chinese traditional concepts were incorporated into Qing imperial family and court official garments through the use of symbolic motifs. These motifs honored the wearers with fortune while demonstrating rank, privilege and political power.

The Chinese Imperial Costume Collection at the University of Hawai'i at Mānoa dates from eighteenth-century China. The collection consists of one official court surcoat (*gunfu* 衮服), four semi-official court robes (*jifu* 吉服), one non-official men's coat (*changfu* 常服), and six non-official ladies' coats (*changyi*, 廠衣), as well as four women's skirts, six square rank badges and some small artifacts, including jewelry and shoes.

This chapter discusses five court garments: one official surcoat and four semi-official robes, which feature the dragon (*long* 龍) (or python (*mang* 蟒) as the central motif, meant to signify the imperial family and nobles.

The dragon is the primary icon of the twelve symbols of sovereignty (十二章紋樣), representing the emperor and imperial authority. Imperial dragon robes were first documented in the Tang Dynasty (618–906). Dragons possessed enormous cultural significance in the Ming Dynasty (1368–1644), which ruled before the Qing Dynasty. The dragon symbolizes *yang* and masculine power. It also represents the East, protection, vigilance, benevolence, prosperity, longevity and renewal of life. Qing emperors maintained the use of the dragon on official costumes to symbolize their conquest and to usher in the new era.

The Qing imperial kinship system includes nine levels down from the emperor as shown in the chart on page 2. The chart on page 3 shows the specific badges for the imperial kinship surcoats that were designed for the respective affinity members.

Dragons are depicted chasing or grasping a flaming pearl. The legend of the dragon and the pearl origi-

皇 QING IMPERIAL FAMILY TREE

Male		Female		
Emperor 皇上		Empress 皇后	First Concubine 貴妃	Concubine 妃
Crown Prince/ Prince of the Blood/ Prince of the First Rank 皇子	First Prince 親王	Kulun Princess 固倫公主	Heshuo Princess 和碩格格	
First Prince/ Prince of a Commandery/ Prince of the second rank 親王	Lord 郡王	Heshuo Princess 和碩格格		
Lord 郡王	Count 貝勒	Heshuo Princess 和碩格格		
Count 貝勒		Duoluo Princess 多羅格格		
Vice Count 貝子		Duoluo Princess 多羅格格		
Duke 鎮國公		Gushan Princess 固山格格		
Vice Duke 輔國公		Unranked Princess 格格		
General of the Third Rank 三等鎮國將軍				

IMPERIAL RANK BADGES
FOR COURT SURCOATS 階

Rank	Badge Shape	Description
Emperor 皇上	Roundel	Four five-clawed front-facing dragon badges on front and back panels and shoulders with sun and moon sovereignty symbols
Crown Prince 皇子	Roundel	Four five-clawed front-facing dragon badges on front and back panels and shoulders
First Prince 親王	Roundel	Two five-clawed front-facing dragon badges on front and back panels and two five-clawed walking dragon roundels on shoulders
Lord 郡王	Roundel	Four five-clawed walking dragon badges on front and back panels and shoulders
Count 貝勒	Roundel	Two four-clawed front-facing python badges on front and back panels
Vice Count 貝子	Roundel	Two five-clawed walking python badges on front and back panels
Duke 鎮國公	Square	Two five-clawed front-facing python badges on front and back panels
Vice Duke 輔國公	Square	Two five-clawed walking python badges on front and back panels
General of the Third Rank 三等鎮國將軍	Square	Two five-clawed walking python badges on front and back panels

nate from the Han Dynasty 漢朝 (206 BCE–220 CE), when it was observed that the moon rose between the horns of the dragon constellation during the Lunar New Year. In Daoism, the flaming pearl stands for spiritual perfection.

The dragon, water, and mountain motifs are present in all five imperial dragon robes in the University of Hawai'i at Mānoa Costume Collection. Water is synonymous with the dragon in the Chinese tradition. The ancient Chinese believed the dragon lived in the mountain and seas. Dragons were thought to breathe wind and create rain. The water and wave motifs appeared only in Qing Dynasty official garments. The wave and water current patterns depict changing tides, which symbolize the flow of energy and the continual movement of life. Additional motifs, such as the eight Buddhist treasures (八寶) are incorporated into the wave patterns. Ancient Chinese believed that mountains were the closest place to the gods. Due to their expanse and height, mountains are also an emblem of limitlessness.

A total of nine dragons are arranged on each of the four *jifu* 吉服 (semi-official court dragon robe) featured in the University of Hawai'i at Mānoa Costume Collection. Due to the locations of the dragons on *jifu*, only five dragons can be seen from either the front or the back panel. This arrangement signifies the "nine-five" concept in Chinese tradition, which symbolizes the power and authority of the wearer (*jiu wu zhi zun* 九五至尊). According to the *Yijing* (*I-Ching* 易經), "nine-five" was adapted in Qing Dynasty imperial costume design to correlate with the dignity of the throne. "Five" (*wu* 五) holds significance with its association to the number of fingers on one hand, while "nine" (*jiu* 九) is the highest single digit and implies eternity.

GUNFU & LONGGUA - SURCOATS

衮 GUNFU & LONGGUA - SURCOATS

Gunfu 衮服 was a formal surcoat worn by the emperor, *longgua* 龍褂 was the formal surcoat worn by imperial princes, and *bufu* 補服 was the formal surcoat worn by officials. These types of surcoat were customarily worn over the *jifu*, or semi-formal robe, in accordance with court official dress regulations. *Gunfu, longgua* and *bufu* are distinguished one from another by the shape and content of the badges. *Gunfu* and *longgua* both have medallion- (roundel-) shaped badges embroidered with a dragon motif; *bufu* have square-shaped badges embroidered with the animal that symbolizes the rank of the official (see pp. 2–3).

Gunfu have a straight side seam with a front center closure with five knotted fasteners, two side-slits, wide sleeve openings, and are dark-colored in either dark blue, black, or brown. When the *gunfu* is worn over the *jifu*, the shoe-sleeve cuffs as well as the wave and water motifs on the bottom of the *jifu* remain exposed. The shoe-sleeve cuffs of the *jifu* are then turned up over the sleeve openings of the *gunfu* to prevent snagging if the wearer is riding on horseback or turned down to cover and protect the hands. An example of a Qing Dynasty *gunfu* designed for the emperor, is shown in the flat sketch from the *Da Qing Hui Dian Shi Li* (大清會典事例) (fig. 1, p. 7).

衮服

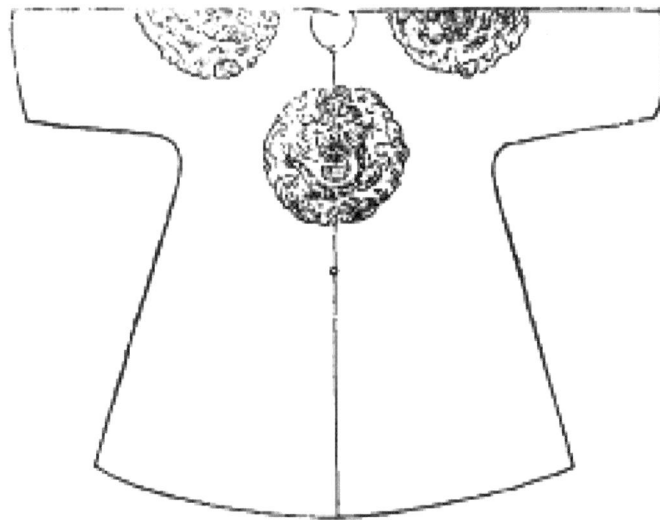

Figure 1. Gunfu flat sketch in the *Da Qing Hui Dian Shi Li* 大清會典事例.

Figure 2. Gunfu 袞服
110.0 cm, 134.4 cm, c.1850–1911 CE
University of Hawaiʻi at Mānoa
Photography by Shu-Hwa Lin.

LINED SURCOAT WITH SLIT TAPESTRY MEDALLION BADGES WITH GOLD DRAGONS & SUN AND MOON MOTIFS

The Emperor's Gunfu

The University of Hawai'i houses one *gunfu* in its collection. The *gunfu* is classified as an Emperor's surcoat, as several motifs in the medallion badges reference the emperor's rank, such as the front-facing five-clawed dragons, sun, moon, and pearl motifs, as well as the gold threads used to weave the dragons and *shou* (壽) symbols. This *gunfu* is made of solid dark blue plain weave silk. Four slit-tapestry (*kesi* 緙絲) medallion badges are located on the shoulders and in the center of the front and back panels.

Sun and Moon

The *yin* and *yang* concept applies to the sun (太陽) (see fig. 6, p. 11) and moon (月亮) (fig. 7, p. 11) motifs on the shoulder badges. The sun represents *yang* and the moon represents *yin*. The sun and moon are sovereignty symbols that were restricted for the Emperor's use only. Garments containing the sun and moon motifs could be worn by other higher ranking members of the imperial family, but only if specially permitted by the Emperor. The sun on the right shoulder badge, depicted by a red disc containing the three-legged sun-bird, is a symbol of enlightenment. The moon on the left shoulder, depicted by a beige disc containing a rabbit mixing the elixir of immortality, is a symbol of heaven.

Pearls

The amount of pearls embedded in the wave patterns of the badges varies. There are fifteen pearls on the front and back panel badges each, eleven pearls on the left shoulder badge, and twelve pearls on the right shoulder badge (see figs. 3 and 4 for examples of hidden pearls under the waves). The sun motif and the odd number of pearls on the left shoulder badge align the badge strongly with the *yang* element. Meanwhile, the moon motif and even number of pearls on the right badge align the badge with the *yin* element.

Clouds

Swirling cloud (*yun,* 雲彩) motifs encircle the design of the medallions. Cloud motifs are highly common to dragon robe design as the dragon is also known as the rain spirit and is associated with the heavens. Embroidered clouds in red, green, grey and yellow decorate the medallion badges. The variance in color signifies changes under control of the power of the emperor and are also an omen for peace. Clouds are thought to bring good fortune because they are the source of rain. The cloud is a homophone for the word 'luck' (*yun* 運).

Shou *Character*

The Chinese character *shou* (壽) is embroided with gold-wrapped threads just above the dragon's head on the front and back panel badges. *Shou* is a stylized symbol constructed using a combination two *ji* (吉, meaning 'auspicious') characters and two *wan* (萬, meaning 'ten-thousand') characters. *Shou* represents infinite prosperity and longevity.

Figure 3. Detail of five-colored weave and *ruyi* cloud.

Figure 4. Detail of sirrus cloud and hidden pearls.

Figure 5. Shou-character constructed using a combination of two *ji* (吉) and *wan* (萬) characters.

Figure 6. Sun with three-legged sun bird.

Figure 7. Moon with rabbit.

Sun and Moon

The sun and moon pair located on the shoulders of the garment above the dragon's head are placed on opposing sides to represent the *yin* and *yang* pairing. The sun and moon are each a symbol of sovereignty. The sun represents *yang*, the dominant, brilliant force, and the moon represents *yin*, the passive, dark force. The sun symbol depicts a three-legged sun-bird inside of a red circular disc and is distinctive motif only found on the emperor's robe. Although the bird strongly resembles a rooster, its having three legs make this animal unique to the sun symbol (see p. 106). The moon symbol is a beige or light-colored circular disc that depicts a jade rabbit using a mortar and pestle, and represents *yin*. According to Chinese legend, the rabbit is identified as the companion of the moon goddess and is preparing the elixir of life.

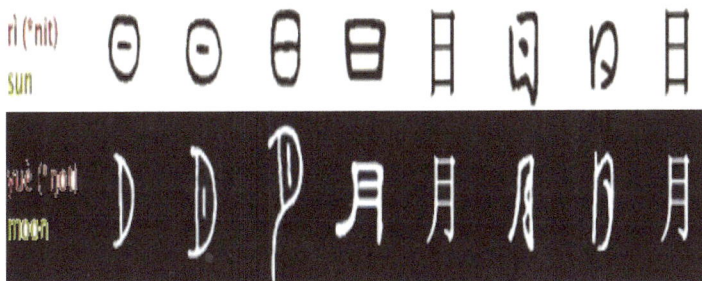

Figure 8. The evolution of the writing of the characters for 'sun' and 'moon.'

Figure 9. Front-facing seated dragon badge.

Numerology and Yin-Yang

Numerology played a significant role in Qing imperial attire as all motifs were deliberately applied in precise quantities. In reference to *yin* and *yang*, even numbers correspond to the *yin* element and odd numbers correspond to the *yang* element. Therefore, an even number of objects represents *yin* and an odd number of objects represents *yang*. To carry a specific representation, each motif may be connected to a number.

Also in the medallion badges are included mountains, waves, peaches, bats, fire, and *wan* (卍) characters. The repetition of a motif may enhance its overall

Figure 10. Close-up view of front-facing seated dragon badge (half).

meaning. Mountains represent places of remoteness, solitude, worship and meditation. Due to their expanse and height, mountains are also an emblem of the limitless. The wave pattern is used to represent the sea, ocean, or water currents. Waves symbolize the flow and movement of energy, the currents of the changing tides,and the movement of life, which is always in motion.

A front-facing seated dragon badge and two half badges were used respectively in the back and front panels. The two front halves were designed for the front opening (see figs. 9 and 11). The badges with sun and moon from the shoulder of the emperor's *gunfu* are depicted on the front and back covers of this book.

The image below shows the bat embroideries cropped out of the medallion. Each medallion has eight red bats, representing "enormous fortune," and four pairs of peaches, representing "longevity." Together, they symbolize the wish for prosperity and longevity (福壽雙全).

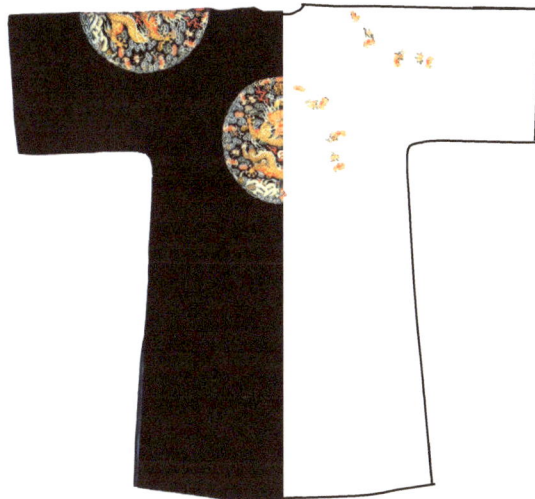

Figure 11. Bats displayed over the surcoat.

Figure 12. Longgua 龍褂; 175 cm x 115.5 cm
China, 19th century
Silk, gold-paper-wrapped thread, leno (gauze) weave, and embroidery
Gift of anonymous donor, 1948 (1138.1)
Photography by Shuzo Uemoto for the Honolulu Museum of Art.

LENO WEAVE SURCOAT WITH SLIT TAPESTRY MEDALLION BADGES WITH DRAGONS

Prince's Summer Longgua

The Honolulu Museum of Art has a dark blue *longgua* made of lightweight leno or gauze-woven fabric. Leno is lightweight gauze-like material using a loosely woven construction. Garments of this open-weave structure were customarily worn in the summer. The *Da Qing Hui Dian* mandated the use of leno material at the peak of the hottest season of the year. The open construction of the weave allows air to circulate and cool the wearer's body during the warmer seasons. According to the *Si Ku Quan Shu*, (四庫全書), this garment was designed to be worn by a Crown Prince.

Medallion Badges

Four five-clawed front-facing dragon medallion badges are embroidered onto the leno fabric on the centerline of the chest and back, as well as on the shoulders of the *gunfu*. The designs of the medallions feature non-ranked motifs, including flowers, peaches, clouds, waves/waters, and bats. The absence of higher ranking motifs, such as the sun and moon, five claws, and front-facing dragon, indicate this leno *longgua* was intended for the rank of Crown Prince.

Yin and *yang* influences in this leno *longgua* are apparent in the inherent symmetry of the designs. Although fewer non-ranked symbols decorate the badges, the motifs contain small variations intended to add subtle complementary elements to the design. For example, the colors, orientation, and size of the chrysanthemum plant on the left side slightly differs from the chrysanthemum on the right side of the medallion. Similar subtleties apply to the remaining motifs. Figure 13 (p. 16) shows a flat sketch and figure 14 (p. 17) is a description of a *longgua* from the *Si Ku Quan Shu*.

皇太子龍褂

欽定四庫全書

皇朝禮器圖式

三十二

Figure 13. Longgua (龍褂) (surcoat for a prince) flat sketch in the *Si Ku Quan Shu, Shi Bu* 四庫全書史部.

16

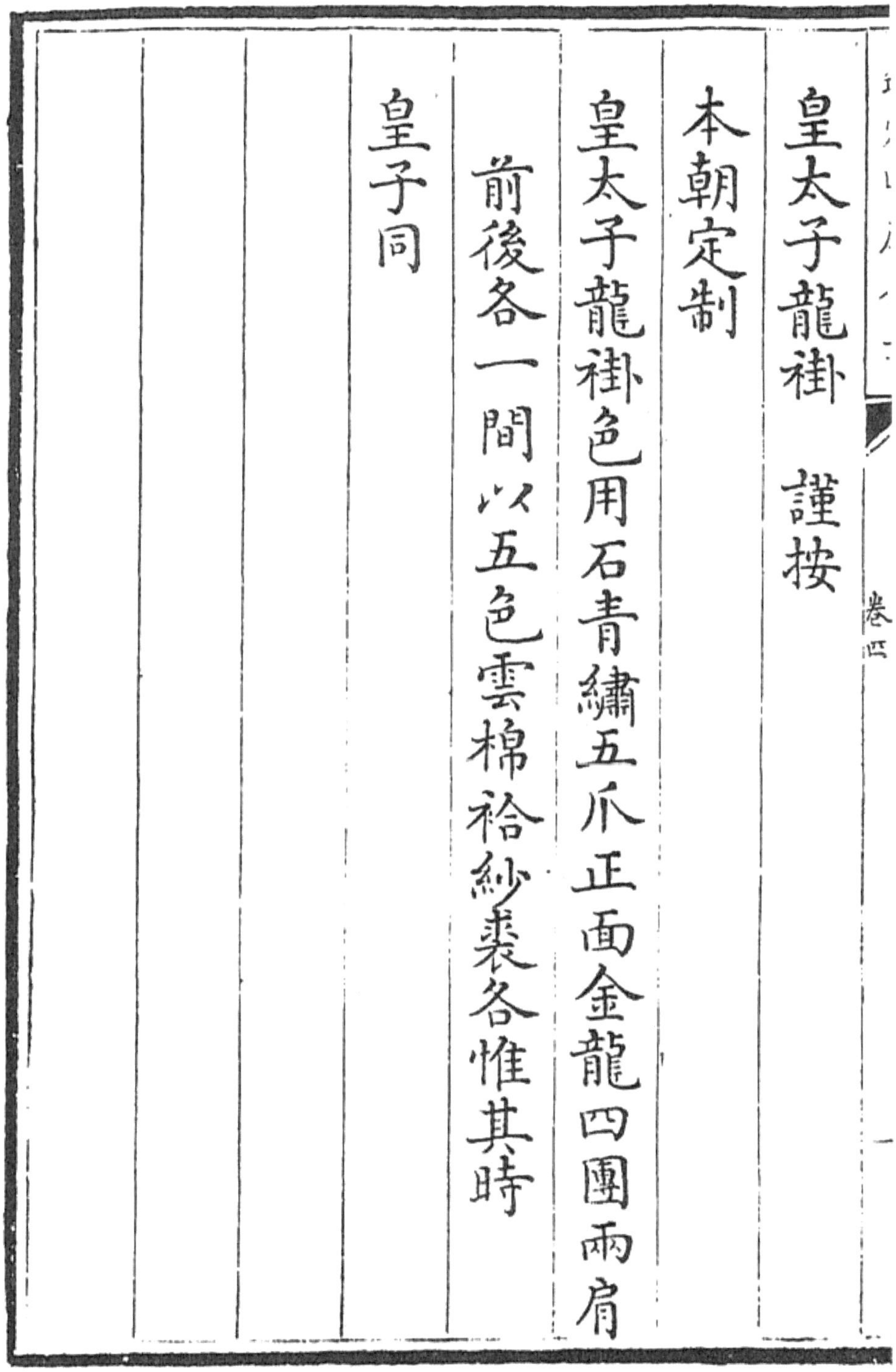

皇太子龍褂 謹按

本朝定制

皇太子龍褂色用石青繡五爪正面金龍四團兩肩

前後各一間以五色雲棉袷紗裘各惟其時

皇子同

Figure 14. Description of a *longgua* (龍褂) for the Qing prince in the *Si Ku Quan Shu, Shi Bu* 四庫全書史部.

Figure 15. Front-facing dragon medallion at back panel of *longgua* (龍褂).
Photography by Shuzo Uemoto for the Honolulu Museum of Art.

Figure 16. Three-medallion displayed on the back panel *longgua* (龍褂).

禳

祚

福

ZHAOPAO - COURT ROBE

Figure 17. Zhaopao 朝袍; 157.5 cm x 210.8 cm China, late-19th century.
Silk, gold-paper-wrapped thread, tapestry (*kesi* or *k'ossu*),
plain weave with supplementary weft, and embroidery.
Gift of Mrs. Charles M. Cooke, 1927 (1063).
Photography by Shuzo Uemoto for the Honolulu Museum of Art.

The bronze, or dark yellow, color of the nine five-clawed dragon *zhaopao* (朝袍) implies the garment was crafted for the third wife of the emperor or the second wife of the crown prince. The *Da Qing Hui Dian* mandated the strict use of various shades of yellow by order of rank. While the emperor and heir apparent were able to don brilliant and golden yellows, darker or less saturated yellow shades, including apricots and browns, were colors permitted for the garments of lesser ranks, including concubines and lower ranking princes.

This bronze *zhaopao* is made primarily of *kesi* and embroidery created with a *wan*-symbol background, except for the collars, hems, and certain sections of the selvages that have been added in order to increase the width at the bottom side-seam of the hem. Repetition of the *wan* 卍 symbol implies continuous blessing. The bronze color of the robe is comprised largely of an embroidered *wan*-symbol background pattern. Two alternating shades of yellow create the *wan*-symbol pattern, representing endless blessings. Because *yin* and

yang are binary elements, the two yellow colors of the patter can indicate *yin* and *yang*. The motifs, including clouds, waves and water, and bats and dragons, are slit-tapestry with painting applied in certain areas, such as the dragon's tails and details of some minor motifs.

Yin and Yang Design in the Principle Motifs
In addition to being a symbol of imperial power and, by virtue, the emperor, the dragon is also a symbol of *yang*. As in many imperial dragon robes, *yin* and *yang* are often demonstrated within the design of the dragon itself. The dragons on the the front bodice of the bronze *zhaopao* show comparatively noticeable differences in coloration and some other design qualities, including line thickness, shape, and object size. Figure 18 (p. 24) shows a flat sketch from the *Da Qing Hui Dian Shi Li* (大清會典事例) of a Qing Dynasty *zhaopao* for the empress. Figure 19 (p. 25) gives details of the dragon and bat motifs on the *zhaopao's* front (above) and back (below) panels.

Figure 18. Zhaopao for the empress, flat sketch in the *Da Qing Hui Dian Shi Li* 大清會典事例.

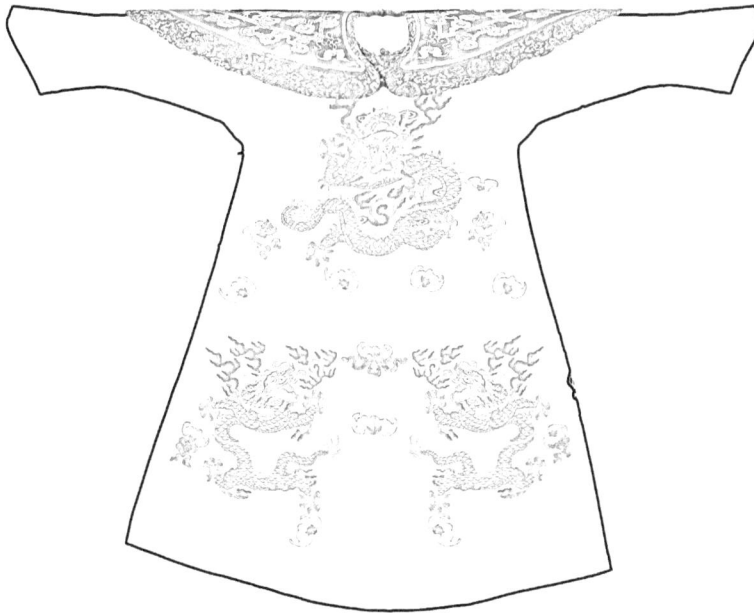

Figure 19. Dragon and bat motif illustrations on front (above) and back (below) panels.

Figure 20. Back panel view of *zhaopao.*
Photography by Shuzo Uemoto for the Honolulu Museum of Art.

Figure 21. Detail of front-facing dragon presented with two-toned eyes with shadowed ears and nose, and two-toned pearl.

Yin-Yang Face

Detecting the differences of *yin* and *yang* elements in Chinese costume design is a matter of relative perception. In reference, the eyes of the front-facing dragon located on the center of the bronze *zhaopao* show the most obvious style differences. On the left side of the dragon's face is a thick brown-colored brow over the eye, and on the right side of the dragon's face is a thick blue line marking the under-eye area. Similar thick blue lines also mark the dragon's face on the right side while thin black lines mark the dragon's face on the left side.

The walking dragons located toward the bottom of the garment also adapt the designs of the center

Two dragons in profile presented with two styles of color tone of eyes with shadow, ears and nose.

Figure 22. Left profile of dragon, walking position.

Figure 23. Right profile of dragon, walking position.

dragon's face, depending on which side they correspond with.

Additional differential design elements on the dragons include the cheeks and ears, which are pink on the left and red on the right, and some slight shade variations in the blue hair and red flames above dragons' heads. The flaming pearl, too, in the center of the

bodice, has a mid-range blue concentric section on the right side that is lighter blue on the left side of the pearl.

Lucky Bats with Wan Symbol
Bats are the second major motif in the bronze *zhao-pao* and are understood to represent luck. Chinese costume design often favors motifs with double mean-

Two-color bats carrying *wan*-symbols with two different colors of ribbons.

Figure 24. Bat biting a *wan*-symbol with ribbon representing blessings through the generations.

Figure 25. Bat carrying a *wan*-symbol with ribbon representing blessings through the generations.

ing. In Chinese, the words 'bat' and 'luck' are both pronounced '*fu*' although the characters are different and have different meanings. Three styles of bats are employed on the bronze *zhaopao*, with 24 bats in total. These bats are depicted flying toward or away from the center dragon, representing the emperor and imperial throne. Seven bats are depicted biting a *wan* symbol laced with ribbons at its tip. This action represents carrying blessings to and from the throne. Three of the bats are depicted carrying the *wan* symbol with ribbons with their feet. Thirteen bats are depicted with empty mouths. The ribbons represent the meaning 'bring' as well as 'generations.' By effect, these bats are also interpreted to signify the passage of power and blessings through the generations of the imperial family. One bat in particular, located toward the below the center dragon on the front bodice carries two *wan*-symbols with ribbons, indicating double blessings and multiple generations.

古蝠獻祥

JIFU – DRAGON ROBES

龍袍加身承天命
以德治天下

JIFU - DRAGON ROBE

The *jifu* (吉服) is a semi-formal court robe or festival dress. Together, the University of Hawai'i and Honolulu Museum of Art house five *jifu* with predominant dragon motifs with rank indicative of the emperor and high-ranking imperial family members. For the purpose of this text, the *jifu* is also referred to as a dragon robe. The rank of a robe can be determined by a combination of factors, including the color, quality of the materials and fabric, and the motifs employed in the design.

Jifu are elaborately designed and colorful garments produced using quality techniques including *kesi* (緙絲) or slit-tapestry weave, leno weave, and embroidery on plain weave silk-satin. As mentioned in the previous section, a *jifu* was to be worn under a *gunfu* as mandated by the regulations of the court official dress in the *Da Qing Hui Dian*. While being worn under the *gunfu*, most of the *jifu* remains hidden from view, except for the sleeve cuffs and the lower portion of the skirt.

The dragon robe includes several recurring motifs, including five- or four-clawed dragons, waves, water, mountains, and clouds, and, in addition, any combination of the Twelve Sovereignty Symbols, the Eight Buddhist Treasures, and the attributes of the Eight Daoist Immortals. The presence of sovereignty symbols directly correlates to the rank of the dragon robe. The use of the full twelve symbols is reserved for the emperor's garments only. The sun and moon symbols are the two symbols of sovereignty specially designated for the rank of the emperor. Fewer sovereignty symbols are used in the design of the dress of lower ranking imperial family members, including princes and high-ranking dukes. The auspicious symbols of the Eight Immortals' Attributes—also called the Eight Treasures, or the Eight Buddhist Emblems—on the robe are meant to bring special well-being or luck to the wearer.

Figure 26. Jifu 吉服; 185.5 cm x 143.5 cm; China, late 18th – early 19th century;
yellow, Silk, gold-paper-wrapped thread,
tapestry (*kesi*) and plain weave with supplementary weft, embroidery accent on dragon's eyes,
Twelve Symbols of Sovereignty.
Gift of Mrs. Charles Adams, 1927 (2119).
Photography by Shuzo Uemoto for the Honolulu Museum of Art.

LINED BRIGHT YELLOW FIVE-CLAWED DRAGON ROBE

The Twelve Symbols of Sovereignty motifs embody the *yin* and *yang* concept in the design of the bright yellow *kesi jifu*. The Symbols of Sovereignty are a minor motif compared to the larger-sized nine five-clawed dragons. However, these minor motifs have a large impact on the overall concept of the costume design. The motifs, no matter how discrete compared to other designs, can be interpreted to have grander "hidden" meaning. It is within the subtleties that viewers may detect the implied and deeper concepts of Chinese costume design.

The dominant motif is the nine five-clawed dragons located on distinct sections of the robe, namely, the front and back center bodice, the front and back lower left and right bodice sides, and on the left and right shoulders, with the ninth dragon "hidden" inside the inner flap of the garment. Two dragons are front-facing while the remaining seven are in walking position. This arrangement of poses are customary to dragon robe design. Each pose indicates the dragon's different power in the various situations. For example, the front-facing (seated) dragon represents the emperor on the throne and the walking dragon describes ascendancy to the throne.

This dragon theme, along with the bright yellow color, regarded as "imperial yellow" or the "emperor's yellow," is the most prestigious of all colors, and the Twelve Symbols of Sovereignty indicate the *jifu* was a first-rank robe intended for the emperor. Although first-rank robes were designated for the emperor, high ranking princes could wear them if specially permitted by the emperor. Additional smaller dragons in walking positions (nine total) line the collar and sleeve cuffs.

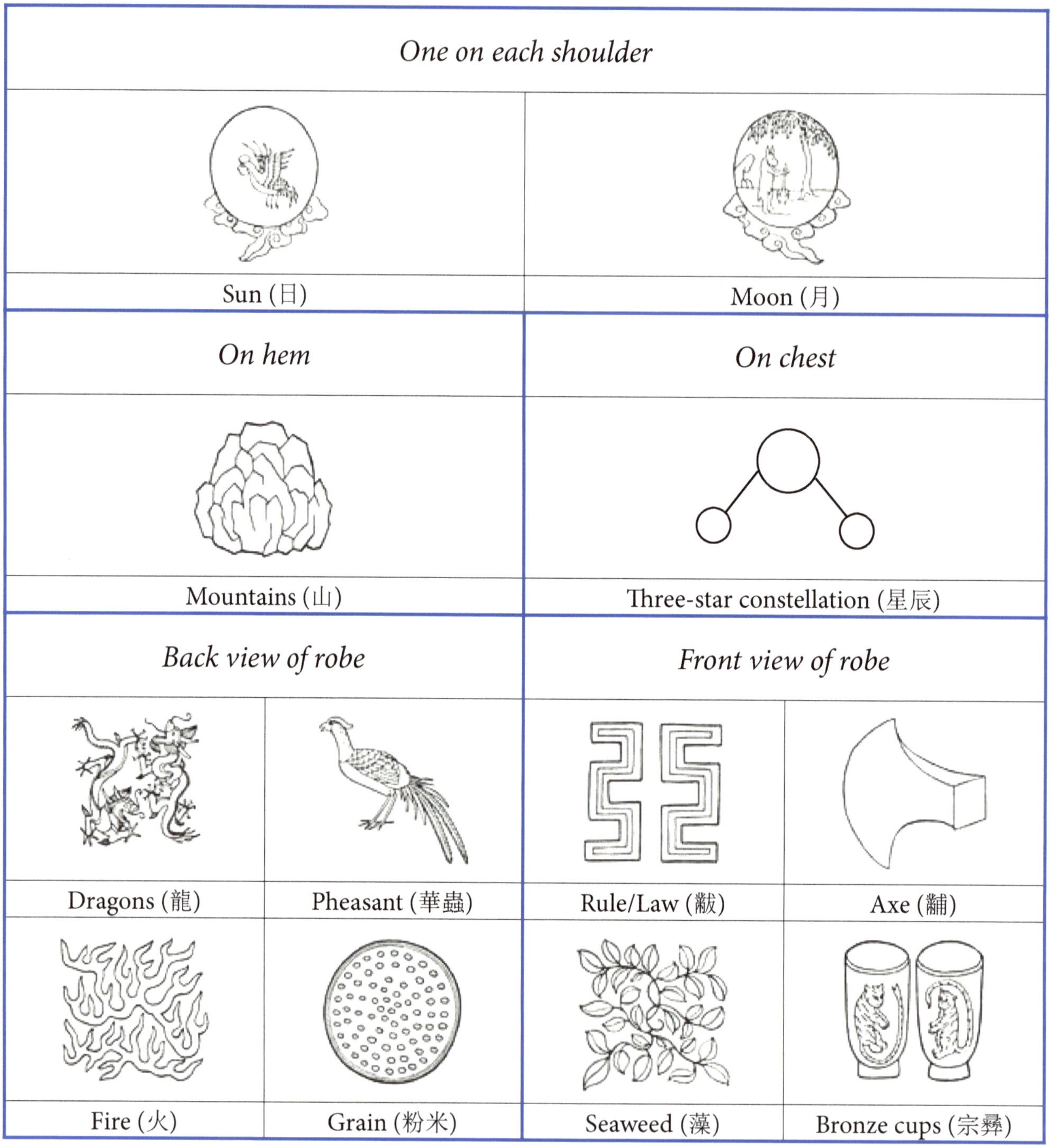

One on each shoulder	
  Sun (日)	 Moon (月)
On hem	*On chest*
  Mountains (山)	 Three-star constellation (星辰)
Back view of robe		*Front view of robe*	
Dragons (龍)	Pheasant (華蟲)	Rule/Law (黻)	Axe (黼)
Fire (火)	Grain (粉米)	Seaweed (藻)	Bronze cups (宗彝)

Figure 27. The Twelve Symbols of Sovereignty frequently seen as motifs on dragon robes with their designated locations on the robe.

Twelve Symbols of Sovereignty Pairs

The appearance and arrangement of the Twelve Symbols of Sovereignty on the bright yellow *jifu* references the *yin* and *yang* concept. In general, paired motifs on Chinese costume may often invoke *yin* and *yang* because the *yin* and *yang* elements are considered a pair. Some symbols are associated with a dominant element. *Yang* is the dominant characteristic of the dragon symbol, for example. For some pairings the dominant element may be relative to the other symbol or position in the design scheme.

Locations and directions for the symbols may connote *yin* and *yang* as well. In the *yin* and *yang* design concept, it is integral to consider, up/down or north/south, left/right or west/east, for example. The arrangement of the symbol pairs doubles the *yin* and *yang* meaning of these symbols. Not only does the pair of dragons and the paired bronze cups with tigers symbolize *yin* and *yang* on their own, but when placed together, strategically, on opposite sides of the garment, they further exemplify the *yin* and *yang* symmetry.

Sun and Moon Pair

The sun and moon pair (figs. 29 & 30) located on the shoulders of the garment above the shoulder dragons' heads are placed on opposing sides to represent *yin* and *yang* pairing. The sun represents *yang*, the dominant, brilliant force, and the moon represents *yin*, the passive, dark force. As was customary for costumes since the Tang Dynasty, the sun symbol depicts the three-legged sun-bird inside a red circular disc. This three-legged bird strongly resembles a rooster; however, the distinctive three legs makes this animal unique to the sun symbol. The moon symbol is a beige or light colored circular disc that depicts a jade rabbit using a mortar and pestle. According to Chinese legend, the rabbit is identified as the companion of the moon goddess and is preparing the elixir of life.

Fu and Axe Pair

The *fu* symbol and the axe (figs. 31 & 32, p. 39), also pronounced "*fu*," play a double meaning on the bright yellow *jifu*. They are positioned diametrically on the

Figure 28. Illustration of the location of eight of the Twelve Symbols of Soverignty on the front panel.

front bodice. The *fu* symbol on the left side of the bodice is a pattern similar to the symmetrical fashion of the *wan* character. *Fu* is made of two mirrored squiggle-shaped symbols. The symbol *fu* is synonymous with lawfulness. The axe symbol on the right side is synonymous with power and force. When paired together these symbols suggests blessings for the people. The *fu* symbol represents blessings upon the kingdom's people by law, and the axe symbol represents blessings upon the people by power.

Seaweed and Bronze Cups Pair
The seaweed and bronze cups pair (figs. 33 & 34, p. 39) are located on the front bodice. On the bottom

Figure 29. Moon (*yue* 月).

Figure 30. Sun (*ri* 日).

Figure 31. Fu (*fu* 黻).

Figure 32. Axe head (*fu* 黼).

Figure 33. Seaweed (*zao* 藻).

Figure 34. Two goblets (*zongyi* 宗彝).

left side of the front bodice is a pair of bronze cups with a painted tiger and monkey. The bronze cups are a symbol of praise to the heavens or gods. The tiger and monkey figures on this robe are painted in simple fashion, however they represent two contrasting ideals. The tiger on the left cup represents dignity and courage, and the monkey on the right cup represents cleverness and flexibility. Upon close observation of the two ani-

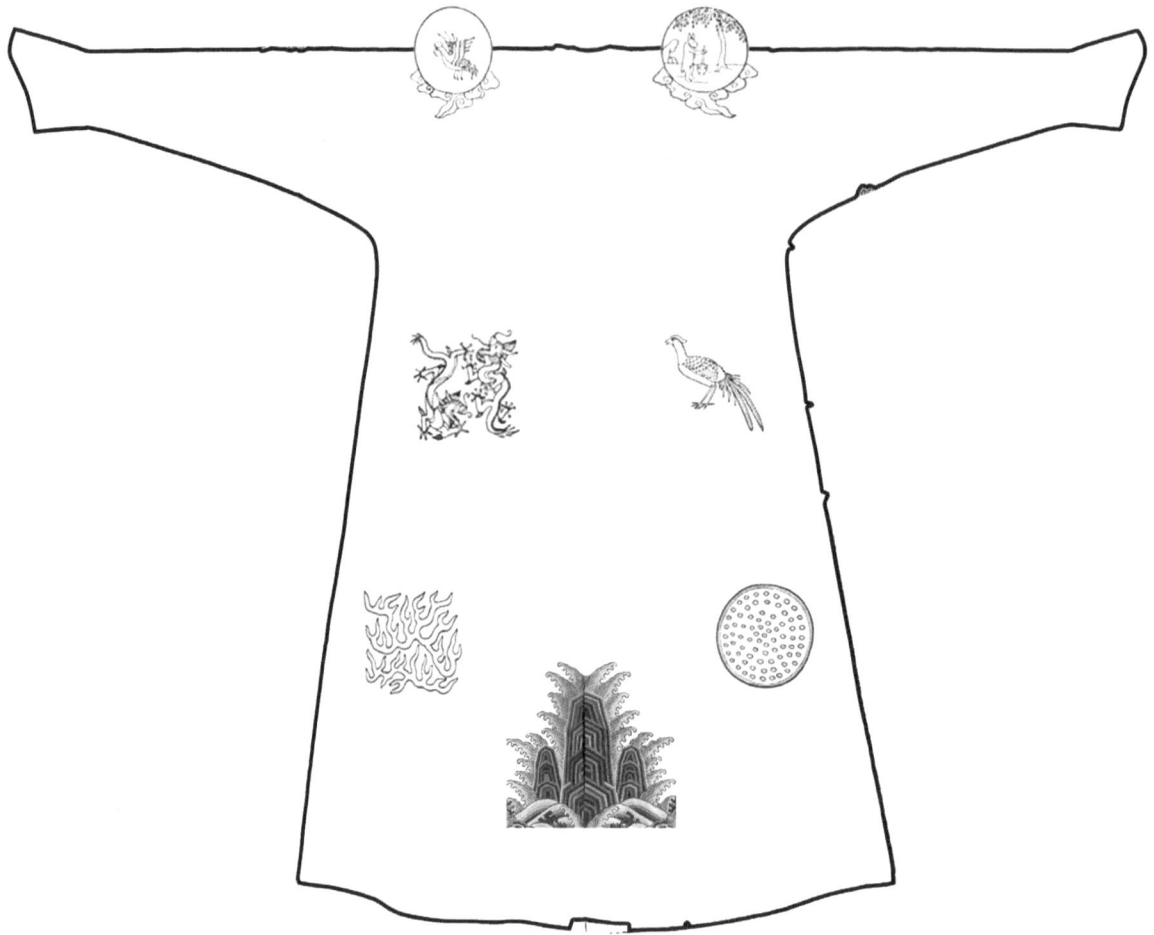

Figure 35. Illustration of location of seven of the Twelve Symbols of Sovereignty displayed on the back panel.

mal figures, their gestures differ slightly in one aspect, that is, the position of the tail. While both animals are upright, the position of the tails is not identical, as one tail curves in front of one of the body and the other curves behind the body. The seaweed symbol is placed in opposition to the bronze cups on the right side of the front bodice. The seaweed is a sovereignty symbol representing progeny and fortune, specifically, that the imperial family may be blessed with many generations. Like the tiger, seaweed symbolizes the *yin* element.

Constellation and Mountains Pair

Another pair of individual sovereignty symbols paired to signify *yin* and *yang* are the constellation and mountain symbols (figs. 36 & 37). The three-starred constellation, located on the front bodice above the center dragon's head, represents the heavens and the *yang* element. The mountains, located on the bottom, represent the earth and the *yin* element. The location of the constellation in the north opposed to the moun-

Figure 36. Constellation of 3 Stars (*xingchen* 星辰).

Figure 37. Mountain (*shan* 山).

Figure 38. Dragon (*long* 龍).

Figure 39. Huachong (*huachong* 華蟲).

Figure 40. Fire (*huo* 火).

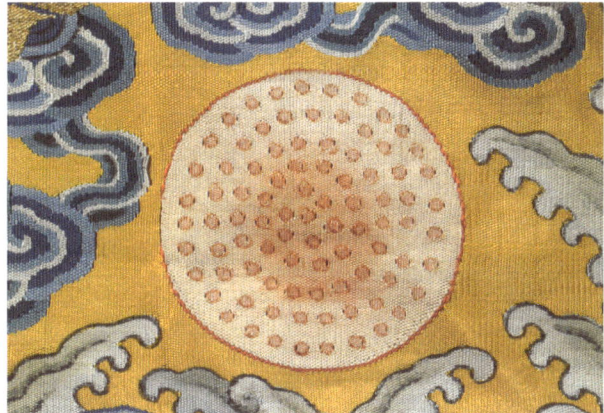
Figure 41. Grain (*fenmi* 粉米).

tains in the south, further emphasize the opposition of *yin* and *yang*.

The motifs on the front side of the robe are in balance with motifs on the backside of the robe. The following symbols are paired on the bodice front to back: *fu*/axe (front top) and dragon/seaweed (back top), bronze cups (front bottom) and fire/grain (back bottom). This opposing arrangement of the symbols of sovereignty pairs further implies *yin* and *yang*. The same design principle also applies to all the other mo-

Figure 42. Back panel view of bright yellow with five-clawed dragon and Twelve Symbols of Sovereignty, *jifu.*
Photography by Shuzo Uemoto for the Honolulu Museum of Art.

tifs, including the primary dragon motifs in which the center front-facing dragon and bottom walking dragons are shown on both front and back sides.

Dragon and Huachong *Pair*

On the left side of the back bodice is a pair of dragons that appear to move in opposing directions from one another. The dragon is a symbol of dignity and courage. The dragons—one ascending and one descending—mirror the Daoist symbol for *yin* and *yang*, which suggests complementary and dynamic action. On the opposite side to the pair of dragons motif is a *huachong* (華蟲, sometimes translated in English as 'pheasant' or 'phoenix'). Like the dragon, this mythological bird is a symbol of the *yang* element. As a pair, the dragons

and the *huachong* are representative of harmony and balance. See fig. 27 (p. 36) and figs. 38 & 39 (p. 41) for images of the dragon and huachong.

Fire and Grain Pair

The fire and grain symbols (figs. 40 & 41, p. 41) are also complementary symbols. Fire is a *yang* symbol that represents creation and progression. Grain is a *yin* symbol that represents safety and security. As symbols of sovereignty, fire suggests the growth and advancement of imperial power and grain suggests the ability of the empire to provide necessities, such as food, for the people. Fire is regarded as a symbol of the force that creates life, whereas grain is regarded as a symbol of the force that sustains life.

Figure 43. Jifu 吉服
c. 1796–1911 CE, 126.0cm x 165.0cm
University of Hawai'i at Mānoa
Photography by Shu-Hwa Lin.

LINED YELLOW SILT-TAPESTRY ROBE WITH COLORED CLOUDS AND NINE SOVEREIGNTY SYMBOLS

Yellow Prince's Robe

The color yellow has represented the emperor and the imperial throne since the Tang dynasty. Different shades of yellow are prescribed to the different designations of imperial rank. Bright yellow, for example, is a color strictly reserved for the Emperor's use, while orange- or brown-yellows are typically worn by the empress and lessor-ranking princes.

The University of Hawaii's yellow dragon robe is constructed with *kesi*, or slit-tapestry weave, with yellow silk-satin sleeves and yellow silk taffeta lining. The yellow theme, as well as the nine five-clawed dragons, nine sovereignty symbols and eight Buddhist symbols, suggest that this robe was designed for a first-degree prince. The neckline trim and shoe-sleeve cuffs are additionally decorated with five-clawed dragons. The repetition of the dragon motifs support the garment's high rank.

Front-Facing Dragon

The dragon and eternal flaming pearl of wisdom motifs show slight variations in detail. Subtle differences in design elements are characteristic of the *yin-yang* dynamic, which celebrates the idea that contrast creates balance. The differences are observed when comparing the front panel motifs to the back panel motifs, or the left side motifs to the right side motifs. For example, the lower teeth of the seated dragon on the front panel are outlined in red on the right side and in blue on the left side, whereas the teeth of the back panel dragon are solid white.

Flaming Pearl

The flaming pearl of the seated dragon on the front panel consists of three colors of rings: a blue disc in the center, a lighter blue ring in the middle, and white ring on the outside. The flaming pearl on the back panel shows the colors in reverse, using a white disc in the center and a dark blue outside ring. Additionally, the flames of the pearl on the front panel are fuller and extend further than the flames of the pearl on the back panel.

Figure 44. Flaming pearl on the robe front.

Walking Dragons

The walking dragons on the bottom two front panels show comparable differences as well. For instance, the blue outline around of the eyes of the walking dragon on the right is heavier than the outline of the eyes of the dragon on the left. On the bottom back panels, the flames surrounding the walking dragons show slight shade and color variations. The flames radiating from the dragons and the pearls on the front panel and on the inner panel are red with pink tips. These colors are reversed on the back panel, where the flames are red with pink tips. A pair of walking dragons were used to present the *yin-yang* concept by using two-toned eyes, ears, horns, and pearls, as shown in figs. 45 and 46.

Figure 45. Left-profile walking dragon.

Figure 46. Right-profile walking dragon.

Kesi ~ *Slit-Tapestry*

The panels are entirely made of slit-tapestry (*kesi*, 緙絲). *Kesi* is a hand-woven tapestry technique used to produce intricate patterns and designs that requires a variety of colored yarns. The *kesi* technique is ideally suited for highly detailed garments such as this yellow dragon robe. All motifs on the bodice were constructed using the tapestry technique, including dragons, wave, water, and mountains, as well as the lattice or maze-like background pattern in blue and gold (a repetition of the *wan* 卍 symbol, which implies continuous blessing). The production of slit-tapestry was time consuming and expensive; a saying from that period went "one inch of *kesi* in exchange of one inch of gold" (一寸刻絲，一寸金). On average, a team of specialized *kesi* artisans required more than two years to complete a single dragon robe. Two-toned teeth, ears, and beards are used to present the *yin-yang* concept, as shown in fig. 47.

Figure 47. Details of close-up picture of front-facing dragon indicated by two-color tone with *yin-yang* eyes, lip, tooth, and ears.

The hidden dragon (the ninth dragon) located on the inner panel of the robe is shown in fig. 48.

Figure 48. The ninth dragon, hidden on the inner panel of the robe depicted in fig. 43.

平

交

龍

Figure 49. Jifu 吉服
131.4 cm x 194.0 cm , c.1796–1911 CE
University of Hawaiʻi at Mānoa
Photography by Shu-Hwa Lin.

LINED BLUE SATIN ROBE EMBROIDERED WITH GOLD DRAGONS AND FLORAL MOTIFS

Gold Nobleman's Robe

Many details of the University of Hawaii's blue silk dragon robe with gold-couched motifs reflect *yin-yang* harmony, from the use of colored threads to the orientation or size of the details. Gold embroidered dragon and floral motifs decorate the University of Hawaii's blue silk dragon robe. The heavy weight of the garment indicates that the threads are made with pure gold, which suggests that the original owner was either wealthy or received this the garmet as a special gift from the imperial family.

Upon closer examination, the gold motifs are couched onto the plain weave silk with either red or yellow thread. The juxtaposition of the yellow and red threads suggest *yin* and *yang*, respectively.

Yellow and Red Threads

The motifs are constructed with five-ply gold-wrapped yellow and red threads applied to silk-satin using yellow and red couch embroidery stitches. Yellow is associated with the earth and *yin* element. The golden tone specifically represents wealth and happiness, and was a color traditionally used in imperial service. Red is associated with the *yang* element; it is regarded as a lucky color to the Chinese, and is used frequently for its associations with good fortune and joy. When both

colors are used in together, they are doubly auspicious. For this reason, this color combination was especially favored in imperial wear. Fig. 50 shows the *yin-yang* face by using two-toned couch stitches and contrasting styles of eyes, nose, lip, and beard.

Figure 50. Two-color tone of couch stitches and eyes indicates a *yin/yang* face.

Dragons

The seated dragon on the center of the bodice is the chief symbol for the *yin-yang* concept as it uses both colors of couching thread. However, only one color is used on either half of the dragon and flaming pearl design in order to exemplify the separation of the *yin* and *yang* forces. On the lower bodice and shoulders, each walking dragon and flaming pearl uses either yel-

51

Figure 51. Yellow couched stitches without shade represent *yin*; orange couched stitches with shadow on the bottom of dragon body represent *yang*.

low or red in association with color of the threads used on the seated dragon. In fig. 51, the dragon body demonstrates two-toned color and design: yellow couched stitches without shade represent *yin*, orange couched stitches with shadow on the bottom of dragon body represent *yang*.

The dragon's eyes and the edge of its body are the only sections of the robe to feature black thread. The *yang* dragons with red couch stitch are highlighted with short-long stitch in black thread on one edge of

dragon's body and beard. All eyes are filled with black satin stitch, encircled with off-white rear backstitch. One eye on the front-facing dragon is made with the vertical satin stitch while the other eye is made with bias satin stitch. The off-white satin stitch highlight around the one eye is formed into a complete circle. The eye is highlighted with two lines of satin stitch. The inner line completely surrounds the eye while the outer line is half complete. As with the dragon's eyes, there are further design differences between the *yin* or

In the two walking dragons in the bottom panel, different style of eyes and shadow represent *yin* and *yang*, here shown in figs. 52 and 53.

Figure 52. Left-profile walking dragon.

Figure 53. Right-profile walking dragon.

yang dragons in places such as the hair, nose, mouth, claws, and patterns of the scales.

Minor Motifs

The red and yellow couch threads are also applied to the wave patterns. The embroidery was applied with five-ply gold-wrapped thread intertwined with red or yellow yarn, further emphasized by yellow or red couch stitch. The two tones of the diagonal stripes in the water pattern were made by alternating the colors of the couch thread and gold-wrapped threads.

The precious objects and the floral motifs, which include peonies, lilies, orchids, chrysanthemums, and the eight Buddhist treasures, are made with five-ply gold wrapped threads with yellow couch stitch only. Peony motifs decorate the neckline and the shoe-sleeve cuffs. Gold-wrapped yarns couched with red thread form the decorative lines around each sleeve. Peony motifs on the robe are shown in figs. 54 and 55, and fig. 56 shows the hidden eight Buddhist treasures poking out of the waves.

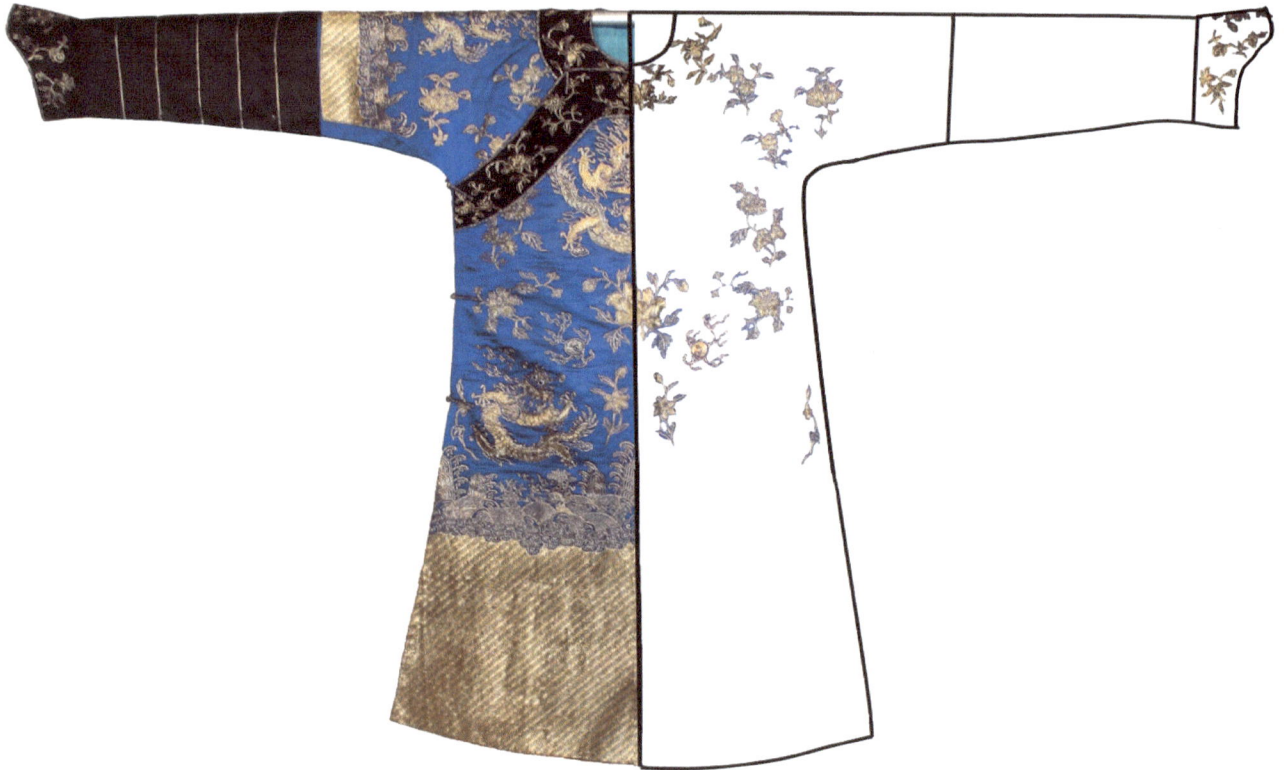

Figure 54. Illustration of the display of peony motifs.

Figure 55. Peony flower.

Figure 56. Hidden eight treasures poking out of the waves.

Figure 57. Jifu 吉服
119.9 cm x 189.0 cm , c. 1796–1911 CE
University of Hawaiʻi at Mānoa
Photography by Shu-Hwa Lin.

LINED SLIT TAPESTRY ROBE WITH FOUR- & FIVE-CLAWED PYTHONS AND PAINTED MOTIFS

The blue *kesi* dragon robe has a mixture of nine four-clawed and five-clawed dragons. The four-clawed dragons are located on the shoulders and inner flap. The remainder of the nine dragons are five-clawed. Four- and three-clawed dragon robes are called *mangpao* (蟒袍). In Chinese, *mang* (蟒), which is loosely translated to English as 'python,' refers a four- or three-clawed dragon. *Mangpao* are differentiated from five-clawed dragon robes, *longpao* (龍袍). In Chinese, *long* means 'dragon.' The detail of claws in the dragons hand differentiates the rank of the garment. The five-clawed dragon belongs to the emperor and first- and second-degree princes. The four-clawed dragon designates dukes and other nobles.

This dragon robe is made with slit-tapestry (*kesi* 緙絲). The slit-tapestry uses white thread on the warp and multi-color threads on the weft. The different colors of threads create the colorful details on the garment. Additional details were painted onto the weave in select areas to enhance the design. Other minor motifs depicting the attributes of the Eight Daoist Immortals, the Eight Precious Objects and the Eight Buddhist Treasures are also featured in the design.

Yin-yang Concept formed by Two-color Toned Motifs
Two-color tones are used to define the *yin* and *yang* principles on this dragon robe. Several of these motifs include bats, lotus, and ribbons. The alternation between the two-color tones not only represent the *yin-yang* concept, but also increase the depth of meaning to each motif. Fig. 58 (p. 58) shows detail of a two-toned front-facing dragon and flaming pearl.

Red and Blue Bats
Bats in red and blue are woven throughout the bodice. Bats (*fu* 蝠) symbolize longevity, prosperity and happiness. The color red represents the active *yang* principle and the color blue represents the passive *yin* principle. The color of the bats possesses a double meaning. In Chinese, the word for 'red,' (*hong* 紅), is a homophone of the word 'vast,' (*hong* 宏). Therefore, the red bats symbolize 'vast fortune and happiness.' Blue is the color of the emperor and, in turn, the heavens. The blue bats therefore symbolize blessings upon the dynasty. See figs. 59 & 60 on p. 59 for examples.

Figure 58. Detail of front-facing dragon and flaming pearl on front panel and two-toned flaming pearl.
Photography by Shu-Hwa Lin.

Figure 59. Red bat.

Figure 60. Blue bat.

Figure 61. Red lotus.

Figure 62. Blue lotus.

Red and Blue Lotus

Similar to the bat motifs, the blue and red lotus design also references *yin-yang* and contains a visual pun. The pronunciation of 'blue lotus,' (*qinglian* 青蓮), is a homophone for the meaning 'clean, upright and free from corruption,' (*qinglian* 清廉). Thus, the blue lotus design has a double meaning and signals honesty and trustworthiness. See figs. 61 & 62 above for examples.

Ribbons

Purple and blue ribbons wrap the precious objects motifs, simulating aura radiating from the objects. The ribbons signify incredible power and, in turn, enhance the meaning of the objects they are associated with in the garment. The Chinese word for ribbon, *dai* 带, has another meaning, 'to bring.' A different word with the same pronunciation, *dai* 代, means 'generations.' When wrapped around precious objects, these ribbons signify the passing on of knowledge and power through the generations. Fig. 63 (p. 60) shows detail of *yin-yang* influenced motifs. Figs. 64 & 65 show the umbrella and gourd motifs. Fig. 66 (p. 61) is a depiction of the placement of Eight Buddhist Treasures motifs on the dragron robe shown in fig. 57 (p. 56).

Figure 63. Detail showing *yin-yang* influenced design motifs: bat, lotus, gourd, with two-color tone.

Figure 64. Umbrella (one of the Eight Buddhist Treasures) with ribbon representing protection.

Figure 65. Gourd (*hulu* 葫蘆) with ribbon representing blessings throughout the generations.

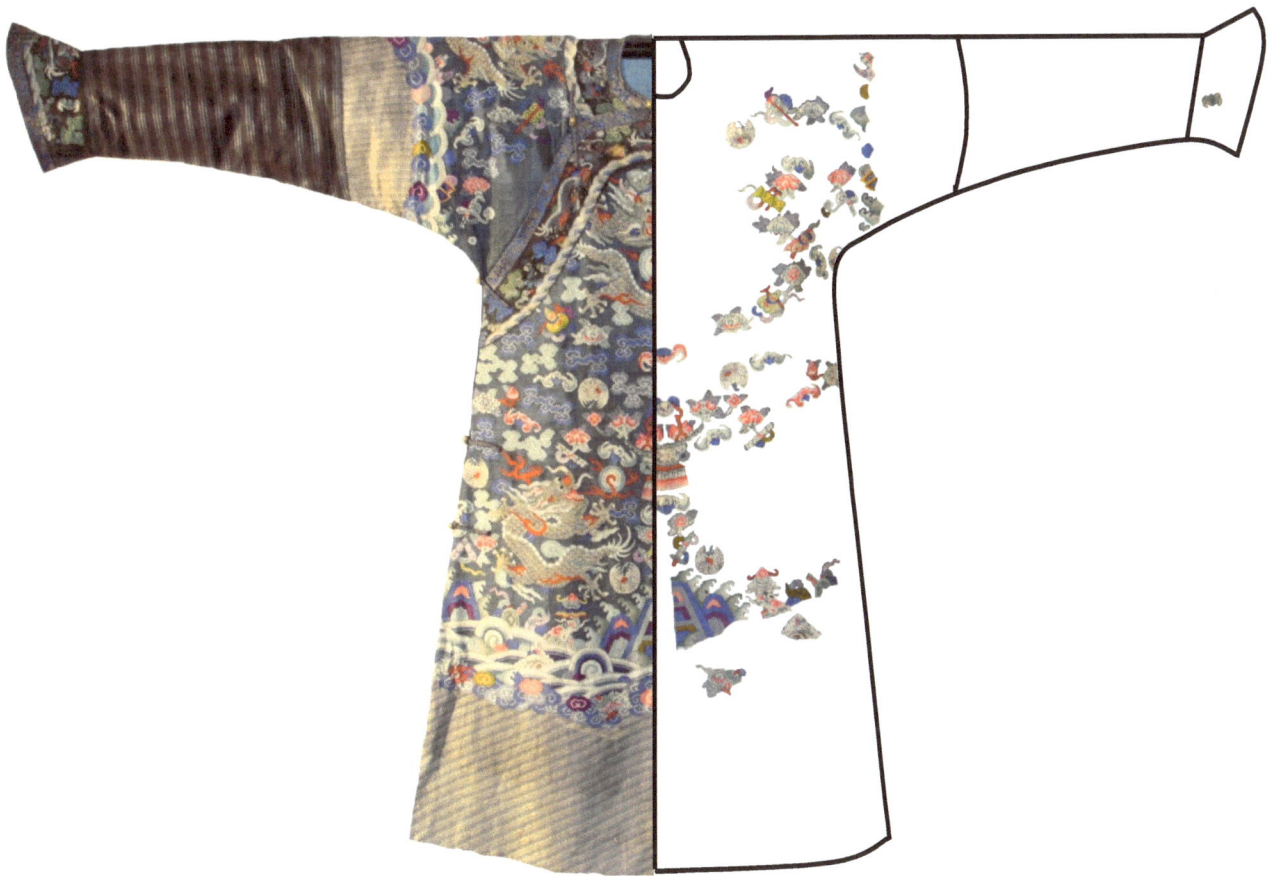

Figure 66. Illustration of the Eight Buddhist Treasures motifs displayed on the dragon robe.

Figure 67. Jifu 吉服
116.2 cm x 143.4 cm
University of Hawaiʻi at Mānoa
Photography by Shu-Hwa Lin.

UNLINED BLUE LENO WEAVE ROBE EMBROIDERED WITH GOLD DRAGONS AND PHEASANTS

Summer Jifu

Imperial robes were designed according to the season. The University of Hawai'i has one summer dragon robe made with sheer blue leno fabric (see fig. 67, and 68 [detail]). Blue leno fabric is used for the bodice and arms the bodice, and black leno is used along the neckline and sleeve cuffs. The border is trimmed with a gold-yellow tapestry made with nine gold-wrapped threads couched into the leno fabric forming diamond patterns.

Leno is a lightweight, air-permeable fabric typically worn in the summer for daytime functions. Compared to the heavier silk dragon robes, the leno woven robe was suited for warm, summer weather, yet maintained the elaborate designs customary to court attire.

In Chinese traditional culture, colors corresponded to the five elements, the directions, and the seasons. Blue was associated with wood, east, spring, and the *yin* element. Blue was also the color associated with heaven and the dragon. During the Qing dynasty, blue was a popular imperial color because the emperor was referred to as "the son of heaven." Blue was also regarded as a symbol of enlightenment.

Dragons

Twelve thread colors were used to embroider the dragon motifs (see fig. 69 [p. 64] for detail). Gold thread

Figure 68. Profiled dragon on leno-weave dragon robe.

63

Figure 69. Front-facing dragon with light shadow, leno-weave dragon robe.

was used to construct the dragon's body. The scales of the body are defined by red and blue stitches. The play of alternating red and blue threads reference *yin* and *yang*, as blue is associated with *yin*, and red is associated with *yang*. There are nine gold five-clawed dragons on the bodice and shoulders, including the hidden dragon on the inside flap. See fig. 69 for details. Five small gold five-clawed dragons also decorate the collar. One additional front-facing dragon is located on each sleeve cuff. The repetition of gold five-clawed dragon motifs and five sovereignty symbols found on this robe is an indication that it was made for a first- or second-degree prince. White storks, also a symbol of sovereignty, are located near each dragon, four in total (see figs. 70, 71, and 72 [p. 65] for detail of stork and dragon motifs).

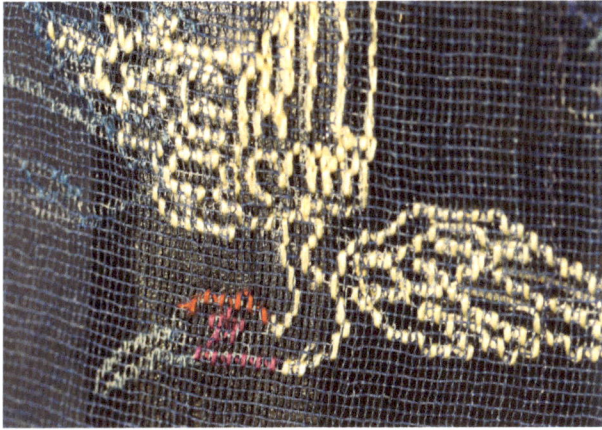

Figure 70. Stork with running stitch on leno-weave dragon robe.

Figure 71. Dragon with *yin-yang* eyes on leno-weave dragon robe.

Figure 72. Front-facing dragon on leno-weave dragon robe.

Several additional differences between the walking dragons on the lower bodice indicates *yin-yang* design. The hair, leg, and body of the left walking dragon are fuller than those of the right walking dragon. Black thread highlights the beard and lower torso of the left dragon, whereas only the beard of the right dragon is highlighted with black thread.

Figure 73. Bat executed in running stitch on leno-weave dragon robe.

Bats

The bats (*fu* 蝠) embroidered along this robe are omens of good fortune (*fu* 福) (see fig. 73 above). Some of these bats are depicted upside down. The Chinese word for 'upside down' (*dao* 倒) is a homophone of the word for 'to have arrived' (*dao* 到). Bats shown flying upside down have the increased auspicious meaning of "good fortune and happiness have arrived."

Vase

Beneath the center front-facing dragon, there is a vase of lotus flowers and bats. The vase is one of the eight Buddhist symbols for peace and harmony, as the Chinese word for 'vase' (*ping* 瓶) has the same pronunciation as the word for 'peaceful' (*ping* 平). The vase possesses unique meanings depending on the kind of flower placed into it. As for this garment, the lotuses and bats imply that "peace brings good fortune and happiness" (和平福自來). Fig. 74 shows the mountains motif executed in two-colored running stitch. Fig. 75 depicts the placement of crane, bat, and immotals symbols motifs.

Figure 74. Mountains executed in running stitch on leno-weave dragon robe.

Figure 75. Illustration of the display of cranes, bats, and immortals symbols.
Photography by Shu-Hwa Lin.

清夏和平

CHANGFU - ORDINARY ROBE

Figure 76. Lined robe of embroidered with eight colored medallions of floral blossoms, 183 x 135.8 cm.
石青大八團花卉夾袍 (清中晚期)
Collection of the University of Hawai'i at Mānoa. Gift of Adelaide Beste, 1977.
Photography by Shu-Hwa Lin.

CHANGFU - ORDINARY ROBE 常

The floral robe shown in fig. 76 contains a mixture of styles, therefore it cannot be classified as official, or as following regalia regulations. It has the mountain and wave motifs on its hem, as found on official dragon robes. However, the horse-hoof cuffs, which are required for official robes, are missing. Non-official robes with eight medallions were popular during the late Qing Dynasty.

Hidden in the wave patterns are the eight-Buddhist treasures, symbols of good fortune, including the conch shell and lotus flower. The pattern of the water current is indicated by diagonal stripes of red, yellow, blue, green and grey, which shift from pale to deep before repeating. The central theme of this floral robe is prosperity and harmony.

The specially selected motifs embroidered on this robe were believed to bring fortune to the emperor and the country. The robe is richly embellished, and reflects the increasing wealth of the Qing Dynasty.

A total of six small and eight large medallions are embroidered on this robe. The large medallions have a single peony at their center. There are 24 floral wreaths that surround each peony. The 24 wreaths represent the 24 solar terms of the Chinese calendar (節氣). Three small medallions are displayed on each sleeve, with one peony flower at their centers. Surrounding each center peony are ten floral wreaths, representing perfection in Chinese culture. The floral wreaths contain smaller peonies, plum blossoms, orchids and daisies. There are also two butterflies in each medallion. All motifs were chosen with the ultimate goal of expressing harmony.

Figure 77. One-and-a-half medallions are visible in this view of the total three medallions located on each sleeve hem.

On this robe, all the small medallions have the same design and arrangement. Inside each small medallion, a medium-sized peony flower is surrounded by butterflies, individual flowers, red buds and wreaths of flowers, including complete wreaths and half wreaths, some partially overlapping. The types of flowers in the small medallion include peony, plum blossom, orchid and daisy. The variety of the colors of the flowers includes red, blue, pink and white. See fig. 77 for the placement and fig. 78 for the detail of the small medallion.

Figure 78. Small floral medallion.

Figure 79. View from front panel of (three full and two half) large floral medallions of the total of eight.

All the large medallions on the robe have the same pattern. Inside the large medallion, there is a big peony flower surrounded by three medium-sized peony flowers, individual flowers, buds, butterflies and wreaths of flowers including complete wreaths and half wreaths, also some partially overlapping. See fig. 79 for the placement and fig. 80 for the detail of the large medallion. The types of flowers in a large medallion include peony, daisy, orchid, plum blossom and *lingzhi* (*Ganoderma lucidum*).

The peony (*mudan* 牡丹) symbolizes wealth, nobility, prosperity, abundance and honor. Since the peony often grows in pairs, so the Chinese relate peony flowers as strings of coins. Therefore, the peony is also called *fuguihua* (富贵花), meaning "flower of wealth and honor."

Figure 80. Large floral medallion containing 24 floral wreaths.

The patterns and arrangement of elements on the left and right sides of the robe are mirrored. However, the colors of the two large medallions located on the left shoulder and left bottom show variation from those of the other three large medallions located on the center, right shoulder and right bottom.

This combination of flowers was an auspicious motif known as "one hundred flowers," which was popular during the Qing Dynasty.

Waves, mountains and rocks motifs are stitched at the cuffs, and hem of this robe. They represent the seas, lands and mountains. The combination of the three motifs symbolizes the hope for peace and harmony of the universe brought by the emperor.

The rocks and the wave are also associated with the phrase "mountains of longevity and oceans of blessings" (壽山福海). See fig. 81 for detail.

Wave patterns embedded with eight Buddhist treasures are embroidered on the bottom hem and on each sleeve of the robe. The patterns of water current are embroidered under the wave patterns of the bottom hem and the sleeves. The pattern of water current is depicted by parallel diagonal lines in five colors: red, yellow, blue, green and grey. Each color of the water current has five variations changing gradually from pale to deep.

Figure 81. Mountains and sea waves.

DAOPAO - DAOIST PRIEST ROBE

Figure 82. Daopao; 122 cm x 165 cm
China, 19th century
Silk, gold-paper-wrapped thread, plain, satin and damask weave, and embroidery.
Bequest of the estate of Ilia V. M. Storme, 1978 (4678.1).
Photography by Shuzo Uemoto for the Honolulu Museum of Art.

DAOPAO - DAOIST PRIEST ROBE 道

Chinese imperial garments were embellished with some of the most intricate, colorful, and diverse illustrative designs, which reflect a strong sense of cultural tradition. The ancient Chinese developed numerous techniques to express and promulgate their cultural beliefs and authority through various artistic media, including fashion and textiles, through the application of symbols, colors, and patterns. *Yin* and *yang* is one such set of beliefs that have been manifested repeatedly since its inception in Daoist philosophy up until the present day.

Interaction and reliance on the heavens and elements played a large part in Daoist practice and was manifested often in the ornate decorations of priestly attire. The intricate designs on this Daoist priest robe illustrate the belief systems observed through natural phenomena with an emphasis on the cosmos and universe. There is no greater symbol of the workings of the universe than encompassed in the *yin-yang* concept, which underlies the duality and harmony of nature and the universe.

Color and Structure

The designs on the Honolulu Museum of Art priest robe (figs. 82, 83, 85, 86) are constructed primarily with gold-wrapped threads in blue and red couched onto silk fabric panels. Yellow was traditionally regarded as the color of the emperor since the Tang Dynasty, and was often used to decorate his clothing, the clothing of high ranking imperial family members, and the imperial palaces and other places of importance to the throne. The color yellow was also used by monks and religious officials; however, they observed the restriction of imperial bright yellow color, which was reserved solely for the emperor, and instead, used dark or brown yellow.

The silk panels on the bodice are blue with a wide red silk border, yellow narrow piping between the red and blue panels, and black binding at the sleeve opening. The contrast created by the blue and red colors suggest *yin* and *yang* respectively. The colors within the gold wrap differ depending on the motifs. Red silk threads are used to couch the gold wrap threads.

Figure 83. Detail showing a dragon descending on Mount Tai.

The priest robe has a comparatively simplified silhouette to the dragon robe or surcoat. It is constructed with long rectangular panels sewn together and draped over the shoulders, covering the body and over the knee. The front opening panel is centered to the body without a one knot fastening for closure.

Tiger and Dragon
A tiger and dragon are depicted on opposing sides of the front panel opening reflecting the cosmic balance of *yin* and *yang* (see fig. 84). The tiger and dragon symbols demonstrate evil and goodness. The orien-

tation of the tiger and dragon figures counteract one another as the figures appear to engage in action. They are also contrasting symbols of power and might. The dragon represents the emperor, benevolence, and imperial strength, whereas the tiger represents courage and dignity, as well as malevolence. Although the tiger is often associated with a negative or evil energy according to ancient Chinese belief, when the tiger (*yin*) element is combined with the benevolent dragon (*yang*) element, they together symbolize harmony and extraordinary luck.

Figure 84. Front view of Daoist priest robe, dragon and tiger are displayed on the front plackard.
Photography by Shuzo Uemoto for the Honolulu Museum of Art.

Figure 85. Illustration of five-mountain symbols, sun moon, 24 constellation, dragons, and pagoda motifs on back panel of the Daoist priest robe.

Figure 86. Detail of lower back panel of Daoist priest robe.
Photography by Shuzo Uemoto for the Honolulu Museum of Art.

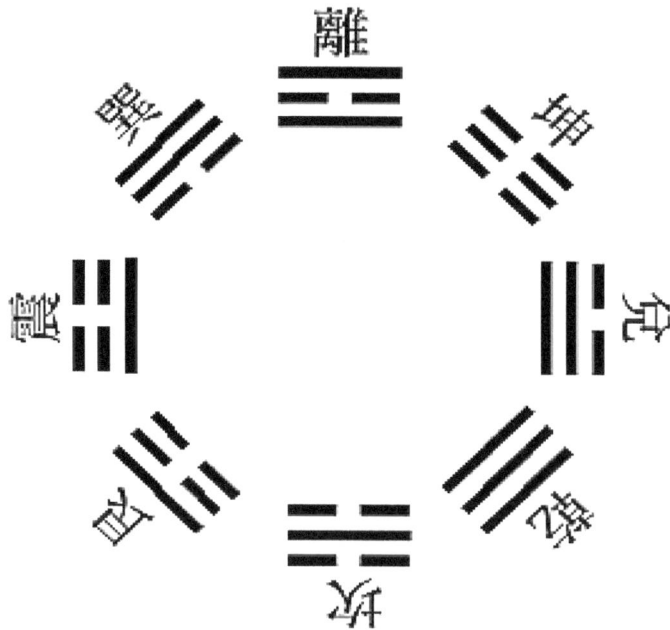

Figure 87. Eight trigrams chart.

Eight Trigrams

The eight trigrams, also known as *bagua*, are a set of diagrams in Daoist practice (see fig. 87). The name 'trigrams' comes from the use of the three broken or unbroken lines in each diagram, representing *yin* or *yang* respectively.

Each trigram represents attributes in nature, whether it be a season, element, direction, personality, family member, or other associated meanings. The attributes represent what are held to be the fundamental principles of reality according to the Dao-ist cosmology, and are shown as a set of interrelated concepts. The eight trigrams are interpreted by two distinct sets of representations, known as the 'Earlier Heaven' and 'Later Heaven' *bagua*. The *Yijing* features 64 possible pairings of the trigrams with commentary on their implications.

Five Daoist Motifs

On the back side of the garment, the design includes the five Daoist motifs, representing the five sacred Daoist mountains 五嶽 and their corresponding car-

Mount Heng (north) 恆山（北嶽）

Mount Hua (west) 華山（西嶽）　　Mount Song (center) 嵩山（中嶽）　　Mount Tai (east) 泰山（東嶽）

Mount Heng (south) 衡山（南嶽）

Figure 88. Detail of the embroidered symbols of the five Daoist mountains from the back of the *daopao*.

dinal directions and elements: Mount Tai 泰山 (east, wood); Mount Heng 衡山 (south, fire); Mount Hua 華山 (west, metal); Mount Heng 恆山 (north, water); and Mount Song 嵩山 (center, earth). (See fig. 88.)

According to Chinese folklore, the mountains originated from the body of Pangu, the first being and creator of the earth. Each mountain represents parts of his body and has special meanings attributed to the location. His head, for example, lies to the east and formed Mount Tai, which is regarded as the most significant place, associated with birth and death.

Pagoda with Pair of Dragons

A large design of a pagoda protected by two four-clawed dragons is shown on the center back of the priest robe. The two large dragons are shown encircling and guarding the pagoda. As the pair of dragons are a symbol of sovereignty representing the emperor, the arrangement may imply that the Daoist priests' faction is under the watchful eye and protection of the emperor.

There are several additional four-clawed dragon arrangements on the robe, which further enforce this point, including the pair of walking dragons on the red silk border as well as the one front facing dragon and accompanying four walking dragons on the blue silk panel. The four-clawed dragons, also referred to as pythons or *mang*, are the symbol for lower ranking officials or priests.

Twenty-four Constellations

Surrounding the pagoda and dragon, the twenty-four constellations represent the solar terms in the Daoist cosmology. The three-star constellation positioned above the design is also a symbol of sovereignty. These twenty-four solar terms represent the scheme and movement of the cosmos, and were important to the Chinese to identify the distinct periods for tending to food crops throughout the year. As with many practical aspects of Chinese life, management of food crops according to the season was practiced within the framework of the Daoist belief system.

Sun and Moon

The sun and moon motifs, two of the twelve symbols of sovereignty, represent *yin* and *yang* respectively. These symbols are placed on either side of the pagoda and paired dragons motif. The sun and moon are one of the most recognizable *yin-yang* symbols, which embody the duality of the contrasting elements and together form balance, such as light/dark and day/night. See figs. 89 & 90.

Eight Treasures

Additional motifs include the fish, umbrella, endless knot, wheel, lotus, and canopy of the Eight Buddhist Treasures. Daoism originated alongside Buddhism, and, as a result, many Daoist and Buddhist symbols and images overlap, such as the Eight Buddhist Treasures.

Figure 89. Detail of moon symbol, left shoulder back panel of Daoist priest robe. *Photography by Shuzo Uemoto for the Honolulu Museum of Art.*

Figure 90. Detail of sun symbol, right shoulder back panel of Daoist priest robe.
Photography by Shuzo Uemoto for the Honolulu Museum of Art.

CONCLUSION 論

This project presents an examination and description of Qing Dynasty imperial robes. I am delighted that the University of Hawai'i at Mānoa Asian Costume Collection houses so many Qing Dynasty imperial costumes. But to fully gain an understanding of the depth of meaning of the motif symbolism, in addition to analyzing the garments in this collection, it required examining several Qing Dynasty costume pieces in a number of other locations and referring to Qing law books. The beauty, elegance and value of these imperial garments are heightened by the symbolism and meaning of the motifs used in their design and complex construction. To have been able to include some important Qing costumes from the Honolulu Museum of Art has greatly enriched the content of this book and broadened my views of Qing Dynasty costume design.

Symbolism of Motifs in Imperial Costume
During the Qing Dynasty, costume design was used as a tool to express the values of the imperial rulers. In their selection of motifs, the design of their garments made ample use of the Chinese language's ease of creating double meanings through the use of rebus and paranomastia ('punning'), which communicated hidden meanings to those who could understand such puzzles. At the same time, these motifs in the form of "word games" also served to imbue the garments

with popular images of harmony, peace, power, loyalty, and favor.

For example, the two contrasting colors of blue and red embody different meanings. The Chinese character for "red" (*hong* 红) has the same pronunciation as the character for "enormous" (*hong* 宏); the Chinese character for "blue" (*qing* 青) has the same pronunciation as the character for "Qing" Dynasty (*qing* 清), which also has the meanings "clean, upright".

When red and blue are applied to specific motifs, such as the bat or the lotus, further hidden meanings are revealed. A blue bat (*qingfu* 青蝠) suggests the meaning 'blessings on the Qing Dynasty (*qingfu* 清福). Likewise, a red bat (*hongfu,* 红蝠) denotes a blessing of "enormous fortune" (*hongfu,* 宏福) (see fig. 59 and 60, p. 59).

The motif of a lotus is another popular motif used to suggest contrasting meanings. A blue lotus (*qinglian* 青蓮) symbolizes uprightness (*qinglian* 清廉), while a red lotus (*honglian* 红蓮) suggests the meaning 'enormous peace' (*honglian* 宏蓮) (see fig. 61 and 62, p. 59).

Another example of the use of color is found in the yin/yang faces of some dragon robes, which can contain blue/red eyes, teeth, and lips (see fig. 47, p. 47). Yin/yang eyes are also presented by different colored eyes and design (see fig. 21, p. 27; and fig. 50, p. 51).

Facial gestures and movement were also used to signify contasting implications. In several of the dragon robes in both the UHM and HMA collections, open/closed eyes are used to represent the yin/yang concept of balance and harmony.

The Chinese word for ribbon is *dai* (帶) which has a meaning of "to bring". *Dai* is also the pronunciation of the word 代, meaning 'generation.' Ribbons are frequently seen attached to motifs, which symbolize the wish that the attribute be continued for generations to generations.

The main objective of this project was to investigate the *yin/yang* influences in the design of Qing imperial dragon robes. As mentioned above, contrasting colors (i.e., blue/red), facial gestures (i.e., closed/open eyes), and motifs (i.e., sun/moon; tiger/dragon) were used to represent yin-yang philosophy.

The twelve symbols of sovereignty were used to represent the emperor. In this book, they are displayed in six-pair under contrasting concept (i.e., sun/moon; mountains and three-star constellation; dragon/pheasant; law/ axe; fire/ grain; and seaweed/ bronze cups; see fig. 27, p. 36).

Five-color groupings were used in different motifs, such as clouds and waves, to represent the meaning of 'luck' and 'harmony.'

My Favorite Masterpiece

Normally, it would take more than two years to finish a *kesi* dragon robe. The bronze, or dark yellow, color of the nine five-clawed dragon *zhaopao* (朝袍) with *kesi* and embroidery is the most amazing robe that I have ever seen. The robe's complicated motifs and *wan*-symbol pattern background embroidery create a three-dimensional effect—truly a stunning design. Graphic design by using many forms of a bat motif was a clever technique. The group of flying bats—busy as bees—convey a story to the viewer, animatedly bringing constant *fu* ('bat'→'blessings') to the emperor. Applying both *kesi* and embroidery techniques in one project—as in the creation of the complex motifs of this garment—would take even longer, perhaps more than three years to finish.

Thoughts for the Future

My dream research project would be something that came out of a fun game I had when visiting a museum with my friends. We each would select one favorite object in the museum that we would wish to own without any restrictions. That way we identified our real favorites and discussed our reasons and values for these preferences. This made our museum visits more fun, as well as more educational.

I would concentrate on Qing Dynasty imperial costumes, gathering them under one roof to display, for example, like the Morning Meeting in front of the Taihe Dian (太和殿) (the Hall of Supreme Harmony in the Forbidden City), in different seasons and during different festivals. Artifacts like Qing Dynasty imperial costumes provide an easy way to study this complicated period in history.

Having the same dream, some researchers suggest that these costumes be scanned in the future as virtual images, so that a display could be easily accessed in virtual three dimensional format, for the benefit of the public and scholars alike.

量 DIMENSIONS OF THE ROBES

Qing Dynasty imperial robes are classified into four categories: *zhaofu* 朝服, *jifu* 吉服, *gunfu* (袞服 for the emperor, *longgua* 龍褂 for princes, or *bufu* 補服 for officials), and *changfu* 常服.

The ten robes discussed in this book are used to illustrate how the motifs embellishing Qing imperial robes were selected according to *yin-yang* philosophical concepts.

The following table lists nine Qing Dynasty Imperial costumes.

Collection	*Gunfu* 袞服	*Zhaofu* 朝服	*Jifu* 吉服	*Changfu* 常服
Honolulu Museum of Art (HMA)	Four five-clawed front-facing, dragon badges, embroidered medallions unlined leno weave *long-gua* 龍褂	Bronze *zhaopao*	Yellow twelve-symbol *kesi jifu*	(not selected for this book)
University of Hawai'i at Mānoa Asian Costume Collection (UHMACC)	Four five-clawed front-facing, dragon badges with sun and moon symbols, lined *kesi gunfu* 袞服		1. Yellow nine-symbol *kesi jifu* 2. Blue satin golden embroidery *jifu* 3. Blue five-claw *kesi jifu* 4. Blue 4-claw *mang* (蟒) leno summer *jifu*	Eight floral medallions *changfu*

Collection	*Daopao* 道袍
Honolulu Museum of Art (HMA)	Gold-wrapped threads in blue and red couched onto satin panels; motifs of tiger and dragon, eight trigrams, five Daoist mountains, sun and moon, 24-constellations, and pagoda.

Illustration of the Dimensions of the Robes

Gunfu 袞服

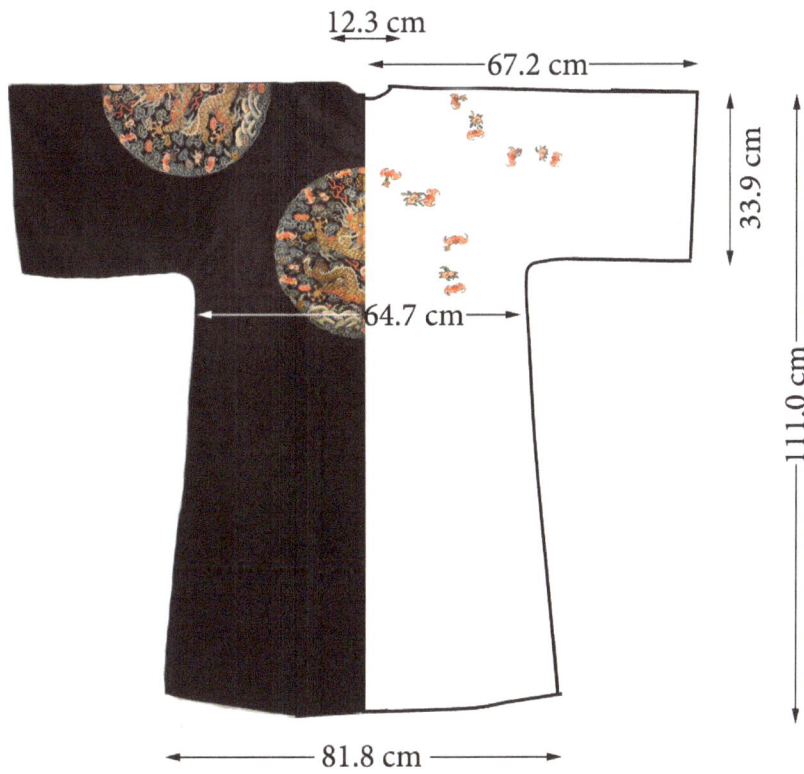

Four slit-tapestry (*kesi* 緙絲) medallion badges are located on the shoulders and in the center of the front and back panels. The front-facing five-clawed dragon and the number of clouds woven into each badge are indicators of high rank. Gold threads were used to weave the dragons and *shou* ('longevity') 壽 symbols. The shoulder badges have either a sun (太陽) or a moon (月亮) motif located above the dragon's head. The sun and moon are two of the twelve symbols of sovereignty restricted for use by the emperor

Longgua 龍褂

115.5 cm

175 cm

Zhaopao 朝袍

This *zhaopao* shows similar characteristics of Manchu imperial attire with nomadic features: a narrow neck opening, a narrow upper part below the arms, and a curved overlapping right front fastened with loops and buttons on the right side of the garment; the two slit hem was a design for female members of the imperial house. This robe's main body was constructed by *kesi* and additional embroidery on the top with 卍 (*swastika,* or *wan*-character 萬字) symbols. Three styles of bats are used to form a rebus with the meaning 'end-less blessings': bats representing luck (福 *fu,* 24), bats biting 卍 symbol with ribbon (12), and bats carrying a 卍 symbol with ribbon (3). Bats and 卍 motifs are frequently depicted with ribbons (a rebus for the meaning 'generations' [帶→代, *dai*]) in this robe. The ribbons signify power and aura. It would take approximately two or three years to finish such a robe, having multiple embellishments, motifs, and decorative attachments.

Emperor's *Jifu* 吉服

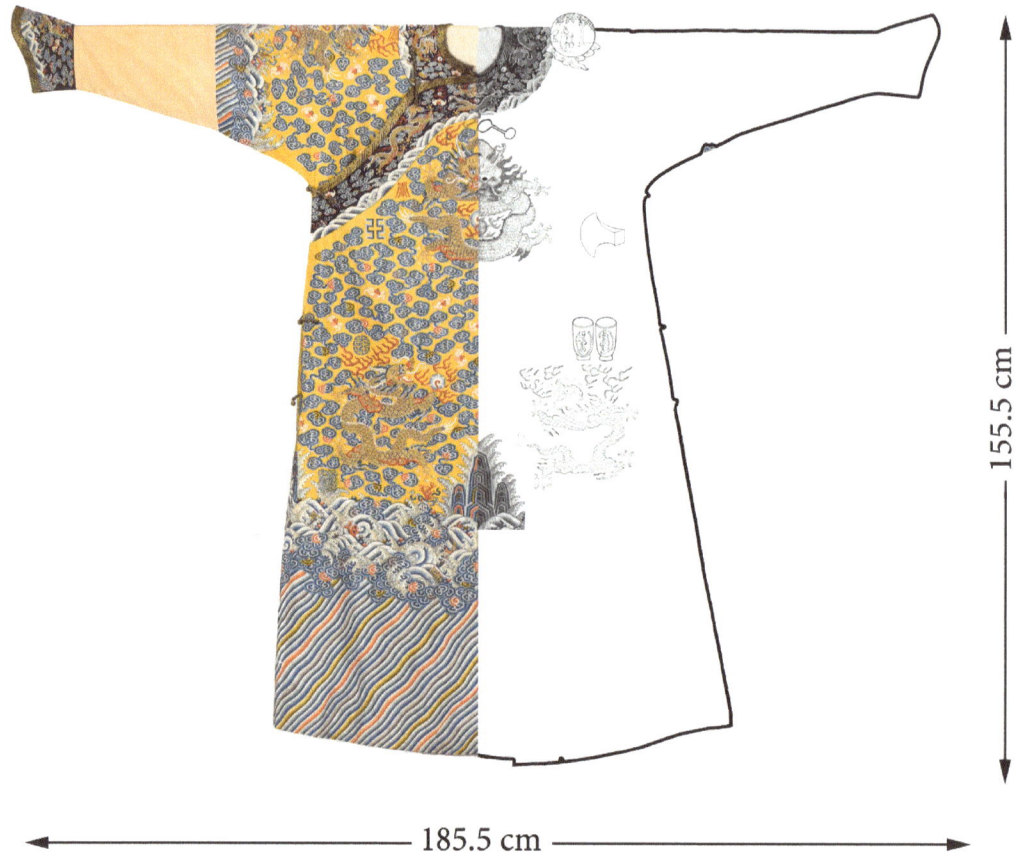

155.5 cm

185.5 cm

A completed set of the Twelve Symbols of Sovereignty. This robe is designed for the Emperor only.

Prince's *Jifu* 吉服

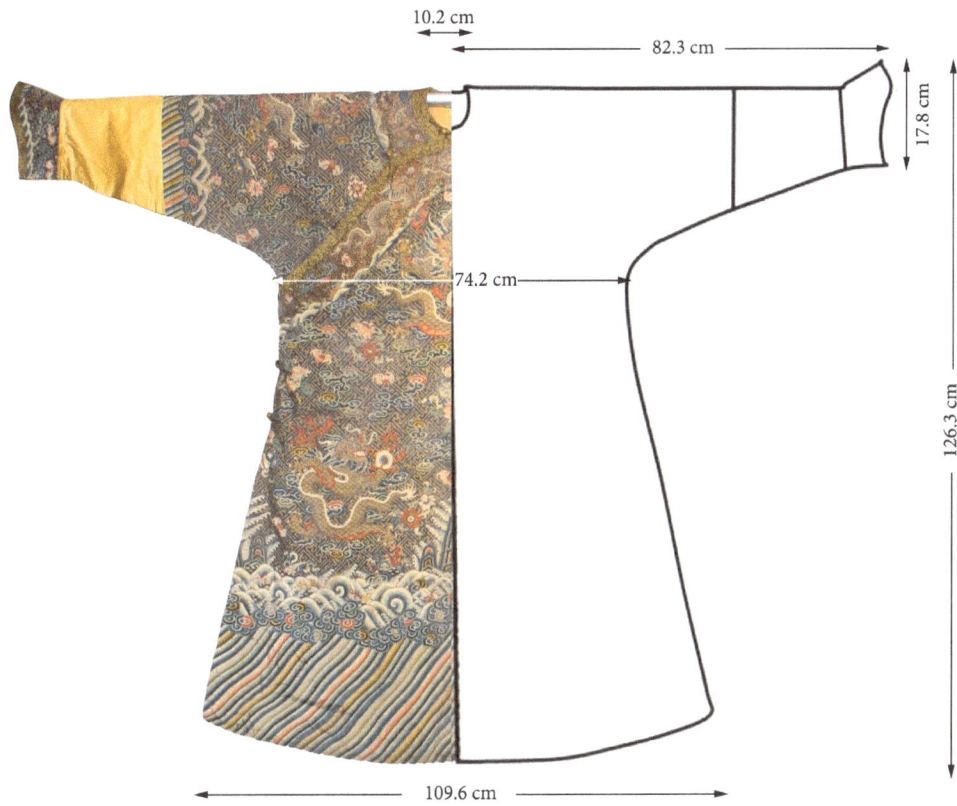

Yellow has been the color of the imperial family since the Tang Dynasty. This *jifu* has yellow satin sleeves and yellow silk taffeta lining. A gold and brown patterned tapestry was used for binding decoration at the sleeve and neckline edges. The yellow theme, as well as the nine five-clawed dragons, nine sovereignty symbols and eight Buddhist symbols, suggests that this *jifu* was designed for a first-degree prince.

Jifu 吉服

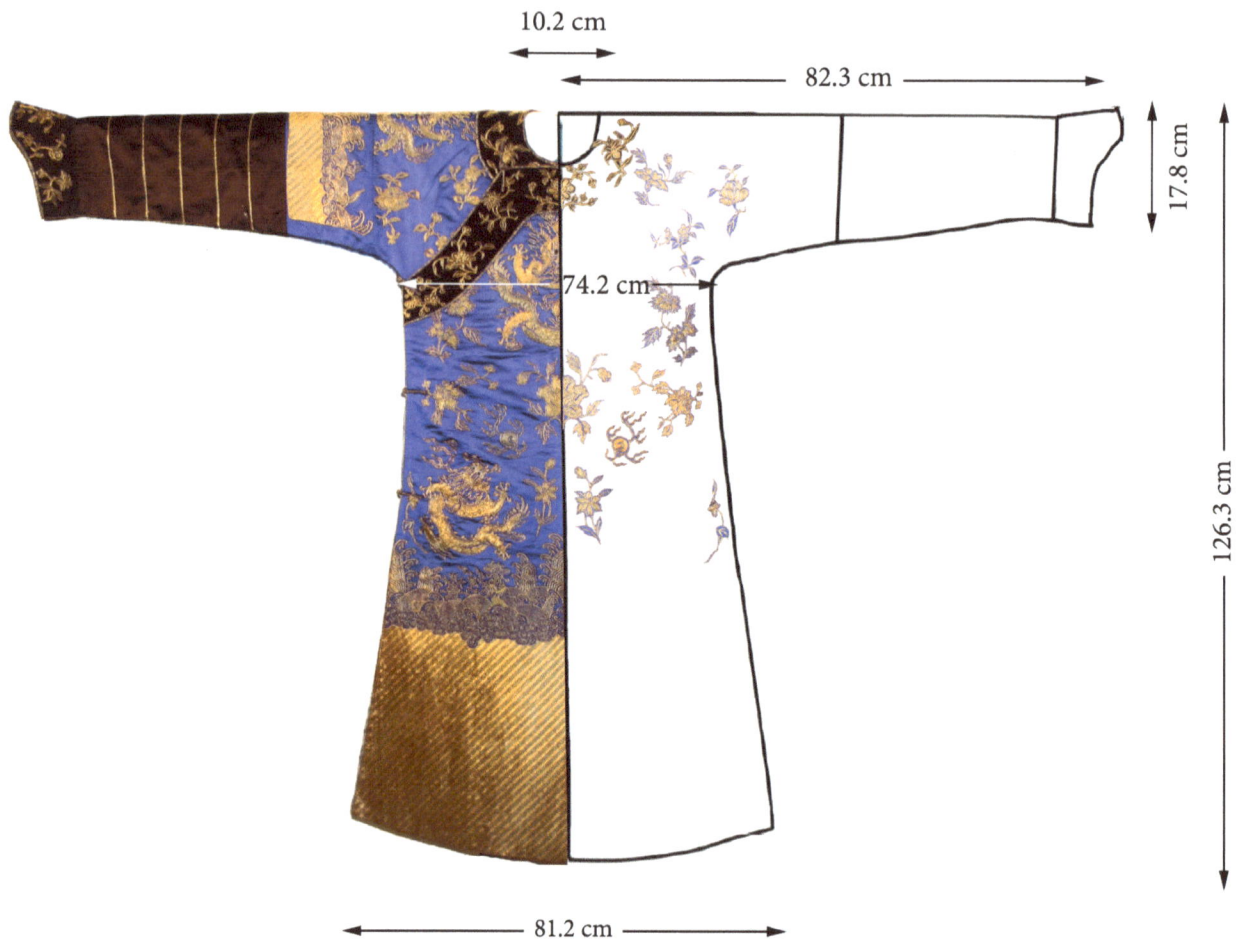

The gold dragon and floral motifs were applied with five-ply gold-wrapped threads and yellow and red couch embroidery stitches. The long sleeves of both robes were cut above the elbow, and the lower portions were replaced with plain or ribbed silk for the ease of bending arms when hunting. The dragon's eyes have different appearances. The off-white satin stitch highlight around the *yang* eye is formed into a complete circle, whereas the *yin* eye is highlighted with two lines of satin stitches. The inner highlight completely surrounds the eye while the outer highlight is half complete. Like the dragon's eyes, there are further design differences between the *yin* or *yang* dragons in places such as the hair, nose, mouth, claws and patterns of the scales.

Jifu 吉服

13.2 cm

71.7 cm

18.3 cm

65.3 cm

116.2 cm

99.6 cm

Imperial robes were designed according to the season. This *jifu* was made with sheer blue leno weave fabric. Leno is a lightweight, air-permeable fabric typically worn in the summer for daytime functions. Compared to the heavier silk dragon robes, the leno woven robe was suited for warmer weather, yet maintained the elaborate designs customary to court attire.

Mangpao 蟒袍

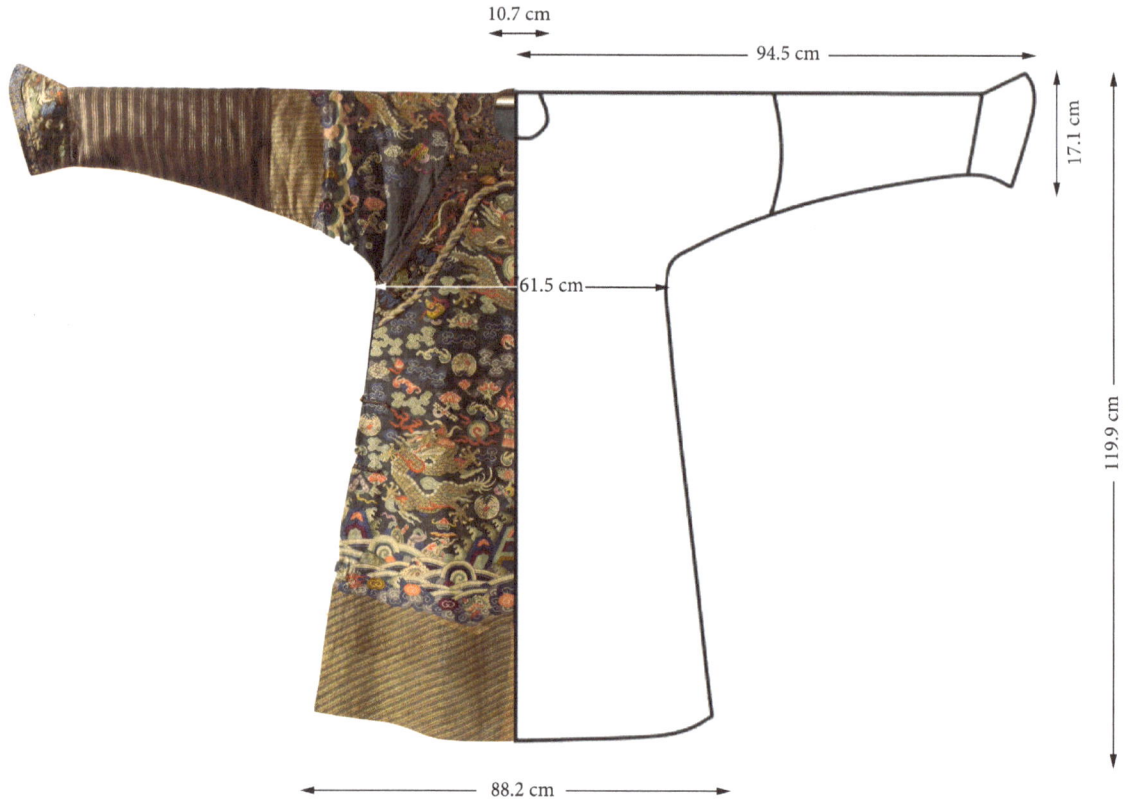

The blue dragon robe has six five-clawed dragons stitched on the bodice and two four-clawed *mang* (蟒) stitched on each shoulder. According to the *Illustrated Precedents for the Ritual Implements of the Imperial Court* (1759), regulations were made to reserve the use of four-clawed *mang* robes to third-rank princes and below, or by high rank officials. The brilliant colors and intricate designs owe to the precision of the priceless hand-woven technique, which took up to several years to complete. And, in some places, additional details were painted on the weave to add color gradation and depth to the design. The motifs include an abundance of symbols of the eight immortals of Daoism, precious objects, and Buddhist treasures.

Changfu 常服

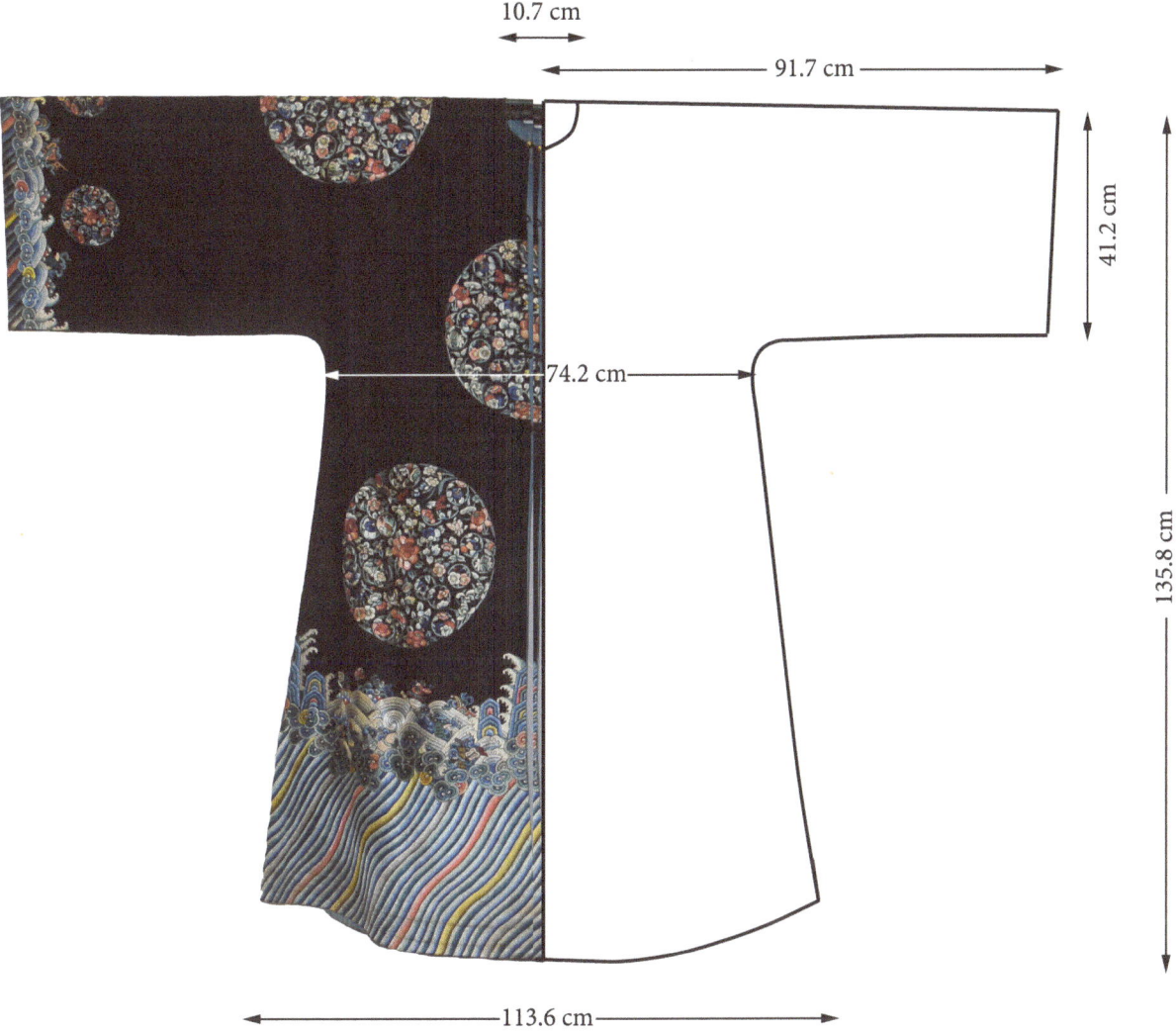

10.7 cm

91.7 cm

41.2 cm

74.2 cm

135.8 cm

113.6 cm

Two alteration lines were found at the hem, which indicates this robe had more than two wearers.

Daopao 道袍

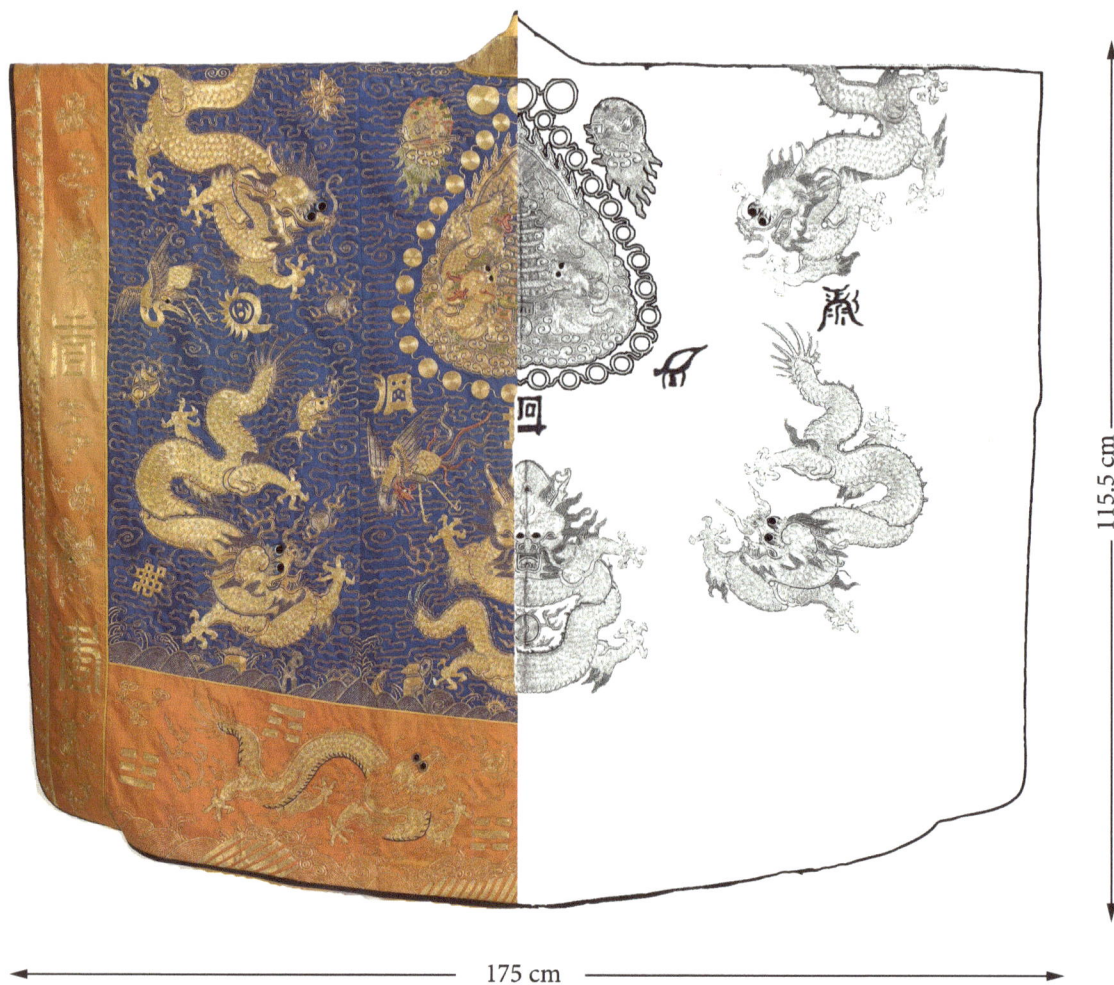

175 cm

115.5 cm

The center back of robe is illustrated with a pagoda covered with the twenty-four constellations, while the front panel displays a paired tiger and dragon, the Eight Trigrams, the Five Daoist Characters, dragons, sun and moon—all motifs representing power. Using gold-wrapped threads in blue and red couched onto satin panels, present many embellishments of power.

CHINESE LITERARY REFERENCES TO MAJOR MOTIFS 詮

BY T. C. YAO, PH.D.

"Wuyue zhenxing tu" (五嶽真行圖)

The *"Wuyue zhenxing tu"* [hereafter, *Wuyue tu*] was a compendium of depictions of the five sacred mountains of China: Mount Tai (泰山) in the east, Mount Heng (衡山) in the south, Mount Hua (華山) in the west, Mount Heng (恆山) in the north, and Mount Song (嵩山) in the center.

Wuyue tu was first mentioned in the *Han Wudi Neizhuan* (Esoteric biography of Emperor Wu of the Han Dynasty [206 BC–220 AD]). Starting from the Han Dynasty, *Wuyue tu* was used by people to seek luck and avoid calamity.

According to Cang Jing (藏經), *Wuyue tu* was closely related to Daoist philosophy. Each of the five sacred mountains had special meanings and representations. The five mountains were associated with the five elements (metal, wood, water, fire and earth), as well as the four spiritual creatures and the earth god in Chinese culture. Following is a summary of their special features according to the following categories: (1) shape, (2) element, (3) representaion of spiritual creatures, and (4) special functions.

Mount Tai: (1) It looks like someone sitting. (2) Wood. (3) Blue Dragon. (4) The drawing of Mount Tai resembles the Chinese character *tian* (天, "sky") or *yu* (雨, "rain"). It symbolizes that heaven is in charge of the life of peole on the earth, including how long they will live and whether they will be rich or poor.

Mount Heng: (1) It looks like someone flying. (2) Fire. (3) Red Bird. (4) The drawing for Mount Heng resembles the shape of a fish, suggesting that things will change. It is in charge of the configurations of the stars and also aquatic animals.

101

Mount Hua: (1) It looks like someone standing. (2) Metal. (3) White Tiger. (4) The drawing of Mount Hua resembles a burning alchemy furnace. It is in charge of all the metals on the earth, as well as birds.

Mount Heng: (1) It looks like someone walking. (2) Water. (3) Black Tortoise. (4) The drawing of Mount Heng resembles a tortoise with legs. It is in charge of the major rivers (江河淮济) (Yangtze, Yellow, Huai and Qi rivers) in China and also beasts with four legs.

Mount Song: (1) It looks like someone laying down. (2) Earth. (3) Earth God. (4) Moung Song is in the center of the five sacred mountains. It is in chage of of the land of the earth, such as mountains, rivers and valleys. It is also in charge of food sources such as sheeps, cows, rice, etc.

Tao-Chung Yao, Ph.D.
Professor of East Asian Language and Literature
University of Hawai'i at Mānoa

Figure 91. "Wuyue zhenxing tu" (五嶽真行圖). Replica of a graphic from a tomb.

Sun Bird and Moon Rabbit

The three-legged gold raven (sun bird) and jack rabbit are animal representations synonomous with the sun and moon in Chinese mythology, as described in various quotations from several historic Chinese texts:

"The sun was depicted as carrying a flying three-legged golden raven." (*Huainanzi: Jingshen, Gaoyou*).「日中有踆鳥。」《淮南子・精神》;「踆，猶蹲也，謂三足烏。」《高誘・注》

"There was a three-legged raven in the sun and a Jade Rabbit in the moon." (*Lunheng: Shuo Ri*, by Wang Chong [Han]) 「日中有三足烏，月中有兔蟾蜍。」後以指日。《漢・王充・論衡・說日》

"Lotus is associated with bird while the golden sun is depicted by a three-legged raven." (*Yue Lu Shan Dao Lin Er Si Xing* [poem], Du Fu, [Tang]) 「蓮花交響共命鳥，牓雙迴三足烏。」《唐・杜甫・岳麓山道林二寺行》

"Three is an odd number associated with yang, *so the sun was depicted with a three-legged raven to symbolizes the* yang *power."* (*Chunqiu yuanming bao*).「陽成於三，故日中有三足烏。」《春秋元命苞》

"The appearance of the black spot on the sun was described as the three-legged raven." (*Wen Zi Meng Qiu*, by Wang Yun [Qing]).「日，日中有黑影，初無定在，即所謂三足烏也。」清，王筠《文字蒙求》

"Some modern Chinese mythologists and astronomers suggest that the middle stroke of the Chinese character for the sun "日", and the middle dot in the ancient Chinese pictograph of the sun ⊖ symbolize a sunspot of the sun or the three-legged raven." 日字中的一橫（在甲骨文中或作黑點），是象徵日中黑子，並認爲三足烏就是指黑子。此說亦爲當代神話學者所繼承，並得到天文學家的支援。

rì (*nit) sun	⊖	⊖	日	日	日	日	日	日
yuè (*ŋot) moon	D	D	ⅅ	月	月	月	月	月

圖 LIST OF FIGURES

Bats with **wan** *symbols:* Bats are the second major motif in the bronze *zhaopao,* and are understood to represent luck. Chinese costume design often favors motifs with double meaning. In Chinese, the words for "bat" and "luck" are pronounced *fu,* although the characters are different and have different definitions. Three styles of bats are employed on the bronze *zhaopao,* 24 bats in total. These bats are described flying toward or away from the direction of center dragon, representing the emperor and imperial throne. Seven bats are depicted biting a *wan* symbol laced with ribbons at its tip. This action represents carrying blessings to and from the throne. Three of the bats are depicted carrying the *wan* symbol with ribbons with their feet. Thirteen bats are depicted with empty mouths. The character (帶) as a noun means 'ribbon,' and as a verb means 'bring'; it is also a homophone for the word 'generations' (代). With all these double meanings, these bats can be read as signifying the passage of power and blessings through the generations of the imperial family. One bat in particular, located toward the center below the center dragon on the front bodice, carries two *wan* symbols with ribbons, which indicates double blessings for generations.

Da Qing Hui Dian Shi (大清會典事): Collected regulations and precedents of the Qing Dynasty.

Dragon (*long* 龍): one of the twelve symbols of sovereignty, representing the emperor and imperial authority.

Eight Buddhist Treasures (八寶): The Eight Auspicious Buddhist Symbols include: Parasol, Conch Shell; Sacred Vase; Royal Banner; Wheel of Life; Pair of Fish; Endless Knot; and Lotus Flower.

Eight Immortals of Daoism (*Baxian* 八仙): The Eight Immortals—Li Tieguai, Zhong Liquan, Zhang Guolao, Lü Dongbin, Han Xiangzi, Cao Guojiu, He Xiangu, and Lan Caihe—are a group of legendary immortals. Each immortal's power could be transferred to a power tool (法器) that could bestow life or destroy evil. The different tool ascribed to each immortal, depicted as a motif, was a stand-in for the depicting the immortal him-/herself.

Gunfu (袞服): an official court surcoat.

Jifu (吉服): an semi-official court robe.

Leno: (*luo* 羅): This weave structure is characterized by a displaced warp whereby the warp is shifted out of parallel position and back again. Gauze can be lacey, open or of a dense structure depending on the degree and method of displacement of the warp ends.

Ruyi (如意): A *ruyi* is a curved decorative object used in Daoist religious ceremony and Chinese folklore, symbolizing power and good fortune.

Slit Tapestry (*kesi* or *k'ossu* 緙絲): The Chinese term for silt-tapestry woven from silk. The design is woven across the width of the textile in a tabby weave binding with discontinuous wefts of the color required for specific design areas. Where there is a vertical abutment of two colors a tiny occurs which distinguishes this weave.

Shou (壽) symbol: a symbol representing "infinite prosperity."

Twelve Symbols of Sovereignty (十二章紋樣): The Twelve Symbols of Sovereignty (十二章紋), representing Chinese imperial authority, have appeared on the five-clawed dragon robes (*longpao* 龍袍) of the emperor since the Western Zhou Dynasty (1050–771 B.C.)

The Twelve Symbols of Sovereignty are the symbolic interpretation of the universe; these symbols of imperial authority assumed a cosmic significance and represented the emperor as the son of heaven and ruler of "All under heaven." The symbols (their numbers accumulated over the years) appeared on the sacrificial robes (*jifu* 吉服 or semi-formal robe) of the emperor:

1. **Sun** (*ri* 日): The sun symbolizes the source of life. In the context of sovereignty, the sun is the symbol of enlightenment and is sometimes depicted by a three legged bird (crow) on a red disc. The three-legged bird is a creature of various mythologies, it inhabits and represents the sun. The sun's active principle is *yang*.

2. **Moon** (*yue* 月): A symbol of heaven. The moon is depicted as a light blue or green disc enclosing the legendary hare (Jade Rabbit) pounding the elixir of immortality. The moon is representative of the passive principle *yin*.

3. **Constellation of Three Stars** (*xingchen* 星辰): The Constellation of Three Stars represents possibly Big Dipper and is a symbol of the cosmic universe. The universe, as personified by the Emperor, is an unending source of pardon and love.

4. **Mountain** (*shan* 山): The mountain is the symbol of the emperor's ability to rule earth and water, a symbol of stability and of the earth itself. (Earth one of the five elements.)

5. **Dragon** (*long* 龍): The five-clawed dragon is the emperor's sacred symbol of imperial power, representing its dignity. The rain divinity is associated with heavenly beneficence and fecundity. Dragons symbolize adaptability as they are capable of transformations; they also symbolize power and

they are the highest symbol of good luck in the animal kingdom.

6. **Huachong** (華蟲): A symbol of literary refinement. Dragons and *huachong* represent the animal and bird kingdoms, hence the whole natural world.

7. **Two Goblets** (*zongyi* 宗彝): A pair of bronze (with tiger/dragon) sacrificial goblets, it is the symbol of imperial loyalty; it also symbolizes the virtue of filial piety. Depicted on the goblets are the two animal kings in the Garden of the Emperor—a tiger or a lion (representing physical strength), and a monkey (cleverness). The tiger is a symbol of the courage to protect and the monkey stands for intelligence. The goblets represents one of the five elements (metal).

8. **Seaweed** (*zao* 藻): Seaweed represents purity, and is a symbol of the emperor's leadership. (Seaweed represents water, one of the five elements.)

9. **Grain** (*fenmi* 粉米): Grain represents the emperors capacity to feed its people, thus it signals prosperity and fertility; meanwhile, it also symbolizes that the emperor is the mainstay for the people.

10. **Fire** (*huo* 火): Fire is one of the five elements and represents the Emperors intellectual brilliance, it also symbolizes the heat. (Fire is one of the five elements)

11. **Axe Head** (*fu* 黼): The Axe stands for 'cut-off' and represents the emperors power to act decisively. It also refers to an axe-shaped pattern used on formal dresses.

12. **Fu Symbol** (*fu* 黻): The bow-shaped *fu* symbol represents collaboration and the knowledge/authority of the emperor to distinguish evil from good, right from wrong. It also is an archaic term for a pattern that is depicted on semi-formal robes.

The Five Elements are represented among the Twelve Symbols of Soverignty by Mountains (earth), Goblets (metal), Seaweed (water), Grain (wood), and Fire (fire).

Wan (卍): a symbol representing "continuous blessing."

Wuxing (五行): The Theory of the Five Elements—often shortened to Five Elements—is the concept in Chinese philosophy conceiving the world as dynamic states, or phases, of constant change.

Yin-yang (陰陽): a concept in Chinese philosophy which describes the natural world by two complementary opposite forces (*yin* and *yang*).

***Yin-yang* Face**: Detecting the differences of *yin* and *yang* elements in Chinese costume design is a matter of relative perception. In reference, the eyes of the front-facing dragon located on the center of the bronze *zhaopao* show the most obvious style differences. On the left side of the dragon's face is a thick brown-colored brow over the eye, and on the right side of the dragon's face is a thick blue line marking the under-eye area. Similar thick blue lines also mark the dragon's face on the right side while thin [black] lines mark the dragon's face on the left side.

The walking dragons located toward the bottom of the garment also adapt the designs of the center dragon's face depending whichever side they correspond with.

Additional differential design elements on the dragons include the cheeks and ears, which are pink on the left and red on the right, as well as some slight shade variations in the blue hair and red flames above dragon's head. The flaming pearl, too, in the center of the bodice has a mid-range blue concentric section on the right side that is lighter blue on the left side of the pearl.

Arts of Asia. (1981). The dress of China in the late Ch'ing dynasty period. *Arts of Asia*. 11(5), 156–156.

Cammann, S. (1979). Costume in China, 1644 to 1912, *Bulletin Philadelphia Museum of Art*. 75 (326), 2–19.

Cammann, S. (1979). Ch'ing dynasty "Mandarin Chains", *Ornament*. 4 (1), 25–29.

Cammann, S. (1952). *China's dragon robes*. New York: The Ronald Press.

Cammann, S. (1950). Imperial dragon robes of the later Ch'ing dynasty, *Oriental Art*. 3(1), 7–16.

Cammann, S. (1944). The development of the mandarin square, *Harvard Journal of Asiatic Studies*. 8, 71–130

Capon, E. (1970). *Chinese court robes in the Victoria and Albert museum*. London: Victoria and Albert Museum.

Choa, S. (1989). *Chinese ancient clothing history*. Tai-pei: Nain–Tan Book.

Fenarld, H.E. (1946). *Chinese court costumes*. Toronto: Royal Ontario Museum of Archaeology.

Garrett, V.M. (1987). *Images of Asia: Traditional Chinese clothing*. Hong Kong: Oxford University Press.

Hanyu, Gao. (1992). *Chinese Textiles Designs*. London: Penguin Book Ltd.

Harris. J. (Ed.). (2004). *China. 5000 years of textiles*. Washington DC: Smithsonian Books. 133–141.

Jackson, Beverly and David Hugus, Ph.D. (1999). *Ladder to the Clouds: Intrigue and Tradition in Chinese Rank*. Berkley: Ten Speed Press.

Lattimore, O. (1935). *Manchuria cradle of conflict*. New York: The Macmillan Co.

Lian, Wong. (Ed. Et al.). *Power dressing: Textiles for Ruler and Priests from the Chris Hall Collection*. Singapore: Asian Civilisations Museum.

Lin, S. (March-June 2008). Chinese court dress design principles. *Context*, 15, 12–15.

Lin, S. (2009). Digitization video of Chinese last empire dress code. In J. Thompson, A. Holden, G. Petersen, & S. Stevens (Eds.), Textile Conservation Special Group special edition, *Postprint*, American Institution for Conservation, 19, 180–183.

Lin, S., (2009). *Threads of majesty: Qing imperial costume collection.* Center of Chinese Studies & Department of Family & Consumer Sciences, University of Hawai'i at Mānoa. (Running time: 27:02 minutes)

Lin, S. (July–October, 2007). Expressions of political rank by textiles: Historic Chinese dragon robes. *Context*, 13, 23–27.

Mattern, J. (1981). *Silk as ceremony: The dress of China in the late Ch'ing dynasty period (1959–1911)*, Fiberarts. 8(3), 75–76.

Michael, F. (1942). *The origin of Manchu rule in China.* Baltimore: The John Hopkins Press.

Rebound, K. (1977). A closer view of early Chinese silks. *Studies in Textile History.* Toronto, Canada: Royal Ontario Museum. 252–280.

Scott, A.C. (1958). *Chinese costume in transition.* Singapore: Donald Moore.

Tortora, P. G., & Merkel, R. S. (1996). *Fairchild's Dictionary of Textiles.* (7th ed.). Newy York: Fairchild Publications.

Stuart, Jan. (ed. Et al.). (2001). *Worshiping the Ancestors: Chinese Commemorative Portraits.* Washington, D.C.: Smithsonian Institution.

Vollmer, J. E. (1983). *Decoding dragons: Status garments in Ch'ing dynasty China.* University of Oregon: Museum of Art.

Vollmer, J.E. (1977a). *In the presence of the dragon throne: Ch'ing dynasty costume (1644–1911) in the Royal Ontario Museum.* Canada: Royal Ontario Museum.

Vollmer, J.E. (1977b). *Clothing and the politics of conquest: Manchu court costume in China.* Rotunda. 10(2), 40–48.

Zhou Xun, G.C. (1988). *5000 years of Chinese costumes.* The Chinese costumes research group of the Shanghai school of traditional opera. (Ed). Hong Kong: China books & Periodicals, Inc.